HEDAKE

HEDAKE

THE TRUE STORY OF THE MAN CALLED HEDAKE
AND HOW THE GAMBLE HE TOOK
IMPACTED BASKETBALL FOREVER

STEVIN "HEDAKE" SMITH

Copyright © 2025 by Stevin H. Smith

All rights reserved. No part of this publication may be replaced, distributed, or transmitted in any form or by any means, including photocopying, recording, or other electronic or mechanical methods, without the prior written permission of the author, except in the brief quotations embodied in critical reviews and certain other noncommercial uses permitted by copyright law.
Permission requests and other inquiries about speaking engagements should be addressed to the following:

G1 Productions LLC
G1productions44@gmail.com

ISBN: 979-8-218-55087-5

This book is a memoir. It reflects the author's present recollections of experiences over time. Neither names or characteristics have been changed, although some events have been compressed, and some dialogue is recreated.

Book Production: Marvin D. Cloud
marvindcloud@gmail.com

DEDICATION

First of all, I express my utmost gratitude to God and my Lord and Savior, Jesus Christ, for granting me the opportunity to share my story. This long journey is also a healing process.

I dedicate this book to my lovely mother, the late Eunice Mae Smith (EMS). Thank you for your ultimate sacrifice in giving me life.

ACKNOWLEDGMENTS

To my cherished wife, DD: I am eternally grateful for the privilege of experiencing life alongside you. Your unconditional love—along with that of our incredible daughters, Aerian, Kayla, and Chloé—has been a source of strength for me. You have stood by me through thick and thin, and I sincerely believe that the best is yet to come.

My heartfelt appreciation goes out to my in-laws, B.G. and Mama Rose, for being two extraordinary individuals in my life. Thank you for your constant support and care for me and my family. I hold the utmost love and respect for both of you.

Uncle Ural, thank you for the continued advice and love you have shown throughout the years.

Cousin Shun, thanks for holding the family down. I really appreciate everything you have done for me.

Momma Daniels, thank you for being the beautiful, loving, adorable woman of God who has shown me nothing but love.

Aunt Lydia, thanks for the love and support you always showed me.

To my man, Mark A. Toliver II; thank you for allowing me to be a part of the N.O.W. Program. We touched many young children's lives through the program.

Coach Leroy Phillips, thank you for giving me a job when I could not get hired anywhere else because of my background. I am blessed to have family members like yourself.

All my family members, I extend a sincere thank you for your unwavering love and support. I cherish each one of you from the depths of my heart.

Mr. Donald "D3" Reid, thank you for all you've done for me. You helped pave the way.

I also like to express my gratitude to New Light Church in Mesquite, Texas, Pastor Shaun and Marian Rabb, for your unfaltering love and support.

I acknowledge every individual who has contributed to my life in a positive manner. Whether you spent quality time with me, gave me an uplifting word, a pat on the back, or heartfelt prayers, I immensely value your kindness.

To EPIC Global Solutions, thank you, Mr. Paul Buck for giving me a once in a lifetime opportunity to tell my story all over the world.

I am deeply indebted to Marvin D. Cloud for his unwavering patience and support throughout this journey. You took the core of my work and transformed it into something greater, enriching my story in ways I could not have imagined. Your dedication and encouragement turned every challenge into a stepping stone, making this experience truly worthwhile. Together, we've reached our goal, and I am profoundly thankful for your partnership.

In conclusion, I urge the reader to delve into the contents of this book. It has not only been a labor of love for me and those involved, but it may serve as an informative and engaging piece that reaches out to a worldwide audience.

HEDAKE Contents

PREFACE	*xii*
PROLOGUE	*xvii*
FOREWORD	*xxi*
INTRODUCTION	1
1: HOW DID I GET HERE?	5
2: MY TESTIMONY	15
3: HE SAW THE BEST IN ME	29
4: NEW THING	47
5: I THANK YOU FOR IT ALL	61
6: WE FALL DOWN	71
7: FEAR IS NOT MY FUTURE	81
8: STAND	91
9: SILVER AND GOLD	103
10: FROM HEDAKE TO INMATE# 01044-748	111
11: THE STORM IS OVER NOW	123
12: PERFECT PEACE	135
13: NEVER WOULD HAVE MADE IT	151
EPILOGUE	167

HEAL EVERY DAY AND KEEP EVOLVING
–Stevin "Hedake" Smith

PREFACE

I consider Stevin as my "little brother." I attended Roosevelt High School in Dallas, Texas, and earned a football and track scholarship to Kansas State. Although I played on the football team, I eventually broke my foot, which ended my sports career. I returned home and became a deputy sheriff and served in that capacity for 16 years.

After coaching Little League Football, I started a youth organization called the The No Opportunities Wasted Program. The N.O.W. Program helps student-athletes navigate through junior high school and high school, assists them in getting college scholarships, and mentors them on their way to becoming good people. I could not have started N.O.W. without Stevin.

Our paths crossed one night when Stevin came out to the Cowboy Sports Cafe with a group of guys. Among them was Kurt Thomas, who played for Texas Christian University and also played with several teams in the NBA, including the Chicago Bulls and Dallas Mavericks.

The next week, Stevin came back. I said, "Hey man, I'm giving a camp."

He said, "Whatever you need me to do; I'll come through." The camp was at Park South YMCA. I had also asked Jeff Fuller and Chet Brooks, who were from the neighborhood to stop by. I wanted to let the children see everybody can get a shot, however, you must follow the blueprint. Jeff played in three Super Bowls and Chet played in two. Jeff mentored me, and I mentored Chet, who was a little younger than us. Also in attendance were Tony and Derrick Battie, who played at Temple and Texas Tech and also played in the league.

Hedake showed up with Sameki Walker, who played for the Dallas Mavericks and the San Antonio Spurs. When he saw the others, he said, "You have the whole neighborhood here." Deion Hunter was my basketball instructor. Stevin saw the connections I had and knew I had a level of trust in the community that came from being more than a deputy sheriff. He was someone from the community who wanted to do good in the community. At the end of the event, Stevin gathered the children, who ranged in age from six to twelve, and had them sit on the floor with him. Then he laid on the floor sideways and beat on the floor.

He said, "Good, better, best; never, never, rest; until your good is better, and your better is best." He had them repeat what he said, and they jumped up and shouted in jubilation. Later, he helped me give away turkeys for Thanksgiving and assisted with a Christmas toy drive.

In time, somebody asked, "Did you see your boy in *Sports Illustrated*?" That's when I found out what was going on, mostly because Stevin participated in a *Sports Illustrated* article. Later, I wrote a letter on his behalf to the judge and told him how involved he was in the program, and everything he did in the community.

After he was sentenced, I continued with our basketball program. I worked to put the team together, and to get athletes from the Metroplex to sign on and commit to speaking, mentoring, etc.

With everything in place, I wrote Stevin a letter: "This is what we are going to do with the N.O.W. program. It will primarily put on basketball camps. We're going to incorporate life skills, and we're going to help young men navigate through junior high school and high school, and get them scholarships. I want you to be my executive of basketball operations."

Mark Toliver

He wrote me back: "Thank you for writing me that letter. It was odd that it came on my birthday. I just wanted to say thank you. It is amazing that a guy like you, would be willing to rock with a guy like me while I'm going through something like this. But whatever you need, when I come home, I'll be ready."

When he made it back to Dallas, he committed himself to the N.O.W. program because he saw the impact he made on the children. We had other mentors, but the connection he had with them was special. He could easily tell his story and say to them, "Don't make this mistake."

I never asked him if he regretted what happened. I believe you always have an opportunity to become who you are. The redeeming factor for him was once he told his story to those young people, it relieved him of a degree of embarrassment or regret. The basketball he played in Pleasant Grove was cool, and what he did at Arizona State was great, and he went all around the world playing this game. But what he did for these young people developed inside of him a long time ago before he even knew it.

God brought Stevin full circle and he knows that. The greatest thing about it, is his recognition of who God made him to be and who he is to God.

—Mark Toliver

PROLOGUE

I had the honor and privilege of watching Stevin "Hedake" Smith blossom into an outstanding basketball player and a tremendous human being. The privilege came from our familial relationship; his mother and my late grandmother are sisters, and that makes us cousins.

Of course, I didn't realize at the time how blessed I was to be raised in the presence of greatness. Hedake and I spent our summers together for most of our lives. Pretty much all our childhood, I was a permanent fixture in his house. Whenever you saw him, you saw me and our cousin, Norron. Tragically, Norron lost his life in 2015, at the young age of 32, during a robbery attempt. May he continue to rest in peace.

I was Hedake's living and breathing shadow back in the day. Although I was on track to play football, it was a natural progression for me to want to follow in his footsteps and learn the game of basketball. Being around him gave me the opportunity to play and practice with such basketball greats as Kurt Thomas, Michael Finley, and Sameki Walker. They all played for the Mavericks. The best part was, I learned from him and developed his one-of-a-kind work ethic. Anyone who has spent enough time with Hedake knows his work ethic has always been top-notch, like the people who surround him.

His life became the blueprint for mine, and I became an outstanding basketball player. I received similar accolades, including being named an All-American in high school in basketball and football. Like him, I also traveled around the world playing basketball in countries like China, Japan, and Israel, even though the NBA didn't draft me.

People find it hard to believe when I tell them that, for years, I didn't know about the trouble Hedake found himself in. We were extremely close and talked about anything and everything—except for the scandal. Rumors were rampant among friends and family in our community, but if it didn't come from Hedake, I didn't believe it or entertain it. That is, until my freshman year at Oklahoma State University, where I earned my basketball scholarship. That's when the truth hit me like a Mack truck.

Coach told us the FBI was coming in to talk to us about life and pitfalls to avoid, as we embarked upon our college careers. OSU's program included cautionary videos and stories for young athletes about college sports.

I always boasted to my teammates, classmates, and anyone else who would listen about Hedake's potential for NBA success. That day, I saw him in one of the FBI videos. And that's when I learned about the ASU point-shaving scandal that featured him dead-center. It was a devastating blow to me and my image of him. I left the room in tears and couldn't wait to get Hedake on the phone to hear from his mouth what happened.

That day, he broke it down to me and explained how he got caught up. We talked about the disappointment he felt, not in the actions that led to him not fulfilling his NBA dream, but how he regretted the fact he let me down. Because of the scandal, he couldn't be there for me the way he wanted to be.

Since then, the scandal is something we rarely speak about, even after the airing of the Netflix documentary, *Bad Sport*. But I am glad that Hedake is finally having his say. My hero, cousin, and "blueprint," knows what he did as a kid doesn't diminish the way I feel about him, his accomplishments, or his influence. Many people feel the same way about the impact he has made on their lives. Despite all of it, I am still extremely proud of him and all he has accomplished in his personal and professional life. And I am blessed to be his little cousin.

—**Byron Eaton**

Top: Byron at Oklahoma State. Bottom: Norron, Stevin, and Byron.

FOREWORD

Over thirty years ago, I had the privilege of meeting Stevin "Hedake" Smith through my dear friend, mentor, and basketball legend, his cousin, the late William "Mookie" Smith. Mookie, an exceptional player from Wilmer-Hutchins High School in Dallas, was someone I looked up to and considered myself blessed to have known and played alongside. When Mookie invited me to watch his "baby cousin" play, I knew there must be something special about him.

Mookie bragged about Hedake, and said, "He plays better than we did at his age." He was absolutely right. Hedake possessed a raw talent, an undeniable passion for the game, and a captivating smile that dazzled the crowd. It was evident that he loved basketball. Even back then, I firmly believed that greatness was in his destiny.

As I spent more time with Hedake, my fondness for him grew immensely. One of my cherished memories was when he challenged me to a one-on-one game. I emerged victorious, but I'll never forget the determined look in his eyes as he stared me down the entire day. He persisted, wanting another chance to defeat me and seek revenge. But I refused, hoping to humble him. I wanted him to experience what it felt like to strive for improvement, as he eventually did.

"You have to beat the best to become the best," I told him. When the Arizona State University scandal occurred when I was playing for the Kings in Sacramento. My first instinct was to call Mookie. We didn't bother delving into the details or questioning Hedake about it. Instead, both Mookie and I were resolute in standing by and supporting Hedake because we knew his heart. After all, neither Mookie nor I were strangers to making mistakes. We all do.

When I discovered Hedake chose to confront his critics and share his side of the story—the truth about what transpired at ASU, I felt a sense of pride. This book, *Hedake*, exemplifies truth and transparency at its finest. Hedake has masterfully guided readers through the challenges he faced and how his faith in God allowed him to rise again.

It takes tremendous courage for a man to open up and share such personal experiences, not only taking ownership of his mistakes but also offering sincere apologies. Many individuals wouldn't have the strength to do so. But then again, Hedake is far from ordinary.

Though my schedule limits our interactions, I occasionally reconnect with the guys from the neighborhood whom I played ball with in the past. We always reminisce about our upbringing in the hood. Every time someone mentions Hedake's name, laughter and joy fill the air because of the immense happiness he brings to people's lives.

God blessed Hedake in extraordinary ways. He bestowed upon him the superpower of exceptional basketball skills and granted him a second chance. Hedake possesses the bravery to share his story and testimonial of redemption with the masses, particularly our youth, to prevent them from following a similar path. That fills me with immense pride.

I am confident that readers will gain valuable insights from this book. I extend my heartfelt wishes to my friend and brother for the continued favor and success bestowed upon him by God.

—Spud Webb

Spud Webb and Stevin.

INTRODUCTION

"Hello?" I tentatively inquired when I answered the phone.

"Hey, Hedake," he said. "It's Joe."

The familiar voice of the longtime stranger on the other end of the line caught me off guard. His voice had aged. It was no longer as menacing as I remembered, and carried a sense of humility that was entirely new to my ears. It was as if this man, too, had faced his own share of trials and was on a similar path towards redemption.

I last spoke to Joe a staggering 30 years ago, and our conversation back then was starkly different. I was oblivious to the profound impact he would have on my life. To be honest, I hadn't cared much, either.

Consumed by the fear of another unexpected knock at the door or a covert ambush, I had avoided asking too many questions about him. After all, I owed the man thousands of dollars. In my early twenties, such concerns haunted my nights.

The day was a warm, partly cloudy, Tuesday afternoon in Texas. The air was sultry enough to warrant turning on the air conditioning in my Toyota Tundra, yet breezy enough to leave the window open slightly. For reasons unknown to me, Joe and I agreed to meet at Saltgrass Steak House in Waco, an hour's drive from my residence. As I cruised down I-35, I welcomed the chance to organize my thoughts and contemplate my opening words to Joe.

I resisted the urge to turn on Pandora and play my favorite gospel tunes, opting instead to use the time for reflection. As I contemplated my upcoming meeting with a man who once caused me great distress, I found myself uncertain of how to greet him. Should I offer him a firm handshake or a brotherly hug? Perhaps a pandemic-appropriate fist bump, or even a blank stare, would better convey my feelings, given our troubled history. These conflicting emotions arose when my college friend, Lester, informed me that the man in question sought to reconnect with me.

The click of a button can unite people, whether or not they want to relink. For me, the prospect of reestablishing contact with Joe meant confronting a past I had worked hard to leave behind. In the aftermath of our initial phone conversation, he flooded me with many apologies and a profound sense of relief. He expressed his desire to meet in person, to offer a genuine apology for the wrongs he had committed in the past.

"I can even come to Dallas, Hedake," he had offered.

The inner conflict within me was palpable. One part of me, Hedake, hesitated, while the other part, Stevin, deliberated upon the offer. This back and forth continued for a while. Hedake instinctively wanted to berate Joe as I did in my thoughts years ago when the Feds arrived at my doorstep. However, Stevin restrained me.

When I thought about it, I understood that being angry with someone who had the same goals I did wasn't right. Both of us sought a swift and effortless profit. As I reflected on my life, I realized I had weathered numerous challenges and traversed through immense darkness. With the dawn of newfound clarity, it would be hypocritical of me to cast blame upon someone else. Ultimately, I chose to accept Joe Gagliano's proposition and arranged to meet with him in person. On my way there, many thoughts traveled through my mind. I eventually grasped the concept of accountability. Admittedly, I knew that accepting the initial offer to shave points was morally questionable. This decision would culminate in the most notorious scandal in the history of college sports. However, who could resist the temptation of earning money while still triumphing in a beloved game? In my circle, I knew of no such individual.

As difficult as it is to admit, I was once profoundly ignorant. During that time, I was not even aware of the meaning of "point-shaving." This term was unfamiliar to someone hailing from my background. My mother earned roughly $30,000 per year, working for Southwestern Bell. In comparison, I could make $20,000 in 40 minutes.

The decision seemed obvious, and while it did not and cannot serve as an excuse, it provides context. The organizers of the scheme assured me I could still win, which was all I needed to hear. I have always been driven by my competitive nature.

Once I arrived at Saltgrass, I felt a sigh of relief and eventually the atmosphere became more relaxed as appetizers and ice-cold water were served. By the end of the evening, we established an unexpected friendship, given our unique individual histories and shared experiences. Forgiving him came easily to me, as I had forgiven myself, long ago.

Journalists, filmmakers, et al, spread false narratives about me, Joe, and other people involved in the scandal over the years. They attempted to portray us as bitter enemies, but the claims lacked merit. Some have even tried to depict me as an uneducated, impoverished individual from a disadvantaged background. Some of that is true. I am, however, far from being uneducated.

People often inquire why, after all these years, have I finally chosen to share my story, especially since many iterations have already been told? The reasoning is straightforward: Just as in basketball, someone must call the play, run the play, and ultimately, make the play.

In my case, God was the one to call the play and that demonstrated His sovereignty and infallibility. The old version of me, Hedake, took charge of running the plays, one of which unfortunately led me to imprisonment. However, in time, I have since forgiven myself for past transgressions and built up the courage to speak my truth. Today, the new, wiser, and more resilient Stevin Smith, executes the plays.

Yes, people have recounted various renditions of my story. The perspectives of Hedake or Stevin have remained untold until this moment. This book provides a platform for me to share my narrative and free myself from the negative impact of this issue. Indeed, *Hedake* serves as my means to clear my name, soothe my conscience, and ultimately, move on.

CHAPTER 1: HOW DID I GET HERE?

We must develop and maintain the capacity to forgive. He who is devoid of the power to forgive is devoid of the power to love.
—**Martin Luther King Jr.**

How did I get here? Those were the words that raced through my mind as I finally came to the reality that the world as I knew it would soon change. It was 1999, and a lot was going on in the US, and around the world. In January, the impeachment trial of President William J. Clinton started. When April came around, the news reported 75 people were dead after NATO accidentally bombed a convoy of Albanian refugees. By July, protests began after an attack on a student dormitory at the University of Tehran. And in November 1999, a trial would take place in Phoenix, Arizona, that would have prolonged effects in college and professional basketball. For years to come, it would influence the world of the multi-billion-dollar gambling industry. It seemed like a script written in Hollywood. And at age 27, I was right in the middle of it. I was an unwitting participant for sure, but still an unwilling star in this blockbuster of a drama.

I have to admit, though; the last few years of my life were a blur. Even my two identities, if you will, Stevin Lamarcus Smith and my alter-ego, Hedake, sometimes clashed with each other. Maybe not in the physical sense, but there was definitely a spiritual battle—even if I didn't fully understand it or embrace it. There was no longer a clear defining line between the two as I wrestled with my different emotions and the what-if scenarios that plagued my thoughts. Today, Monday, November 15, 1999, to paraphrase President Franklin D. Roosevelt, would be "a date that would always live in infamy." It would be a date to choose my fate and challenge my faith. Would I remain a free man? Able to pursue the one thing that made me happy, the one thing I was born to do? Or would they confine me behind bars for the next five years like a common criminal? For real? Sixty full months? One thousand, eight hundred and twenty-five days?

Now, I found myself in a place I could not have imagined. Not even my single-parent mother, my father, other family members, coaches, and supporters saw it coming or visualized it for me. These were people who had my best interests at heart. They had prayed, pushed, and pulled me, to keep me from becoming a statistic. Society had plans for me as a young black boy, being raised in a household without a father. I had already risen above societal expectations. According to those who study such things, I surpassed two of its idioms; first, I wasn't dead. Second, up to the time five years ago when the FBI came to my door, no police agency had ever arrested me. No one in my inner circle ever expected any criminal conviction against me. Nothing. It wasn't in my character. And that's the rub. People will define you by one misstep. It would take a long time for me to understand your definition of me is not who I am.

The question echoed, *How did I get here?* It's not being conceited to say I was once on the cusp of almost every boy's dream. From where I came from, the inner-city of South Dallas, Texas, much like all other cities in the US, many young males aspired to be rappers. However, a lot of us wanted to be professional athletes. We all dreamed of mansions, clothes, and cars. Regardless, it was our ticket out of our lower-income communities and the trappings that often came with the environment. Also it was a chance to make something out of ourselves, and an opportunity for most of us to buy our mamas a home. But as people are fond of saying, "You see the glory, but you don't know the story."

Truth is, the odds are not in favor of many of the boys with stars in their eyes who throw or catch a football; bat or catch a baseball; or dribble or shoot a basketball. However, they don't have that information. They don't understand that only 1.2% of college-level players will get drafted to the NFL; about 10.5 percent of NCAA senior baseball players, will get drafted by the MLB; and for basketball, there is only a .03 chance of a pro career. Perhaps that's why it's hard to get people to see the vision you have for yourself; if we knew the prospects, maybe we couldn't see it ourselves.

Playing in the NBA wasn't a pipe dream for me; it was my reality backed by a sense of purpose, predestination, and possibility. Since I first saw the game on television, before I knew what a basketball was, or held it in my hand, I was hooked. I grew up and worked to develop my game. Every free throw, every shot from the corner, and every three-point attempt, laid another brick towards the building of my sports legacy's foundation.

Ultimately, in my mind, it would lead to me being crowned the king of basketball. Please know I wasn't delusional. I'm not a has-been from high school who only talks about one game-winning shot he made years ago. My resume speaks for itself:

Selected twice to the First Team All-Pac-10. Finished my college career as Arizona State University's all-time leading scorer, steals leader, and most three-pointers made in a career. Selected as All-American. Captain of the USA Under 22 Squad in 1993 that captured the gold medal. Depending on whom you talked to, they slated me to be a first-round pick or a second-round steal for some team in the 1994 National Basketball Association draft. Either way, playing in the NBA would mean the early morning or late-night practice, the drops of sweat, and pushing past the pain of fatigue, or muscle cramps, would now be well worth it. It's called the "no pain no gain" effect.

In 1982, fitness guru Jane Fonda came up with the concept of "no pain no gain," which emphasizes the value of hard work. The term suggests that effort and dedication are prerequisites for success. It further allows that meaningful rewards are only attainable through significant effort, and genuine achievement requires perseverance and determination.

In other words, no one hands success to us on a silver platter. We must work hard to achieve our goals. My mother ingrained that in me at an early age. And although I never actually had a job growing up, I transferred that idea to the basketball court, and it gave me a singular mind for my NBA aspirations. My mother, my single-parent, work-as-hard-as-I-can, mom, taught me in no certain terms to set my goals and work for what I wanted. In the words of the late soul singer, James Brown, "I don't want nobody to give me nothing; open the door and I'll get it myself."

Basketball opened the door and the 1994 draft was the elevator behind it that would take me straight to the top floor. I was in good company. The early 1990s' draft classes consisted of Derrick Coleman, Gary Payton, and Chris Jackson, 1990; Larry Johnson, Kenny Anderson, and Dikembe Mutombo, 1991; Shaquille O'Neal, Alonzo Mourning, and Christian Laettner, 1992; and Chris Webber, Penny Hardaway, and Vin

Baker in 1993. But 1994 would be my time to shine. Among my contemporaries that year were Glenn Robinson, Jason Kidd, Grant Hill, Donvell Marshall, and Juwan Howard. As a point of reference, the Milwaukee Bucks selected Robinson as the number one draft pick and signed him to a 10-year, $68 million contract.

Maybe now you see why that question came to me repeatedly. *How did I get here?*

Ironically, I did everything I could to stay out of trouble from the time I stepped on a basketball court. I didn't use or sell drugs, nor did I steal or rob. I also didn't need the family nucleus of a gang. And in Dallas, there were plenty of them. In fact, in 1990, the office of Texas Attorney General Jim Mattox reported Dallas had 221 gangs, more than any other city in the state. This earned Dallas the dubious distinction of being the "Murder capital of Texas." It was enough for me that everyone I knew wished me well and wanted me to succeed. But now, it seemed like the thing I feared the most would overtake me.

The presiding judge, Robert C. Broomfield was stern and stoic. President Ronald Reagan appointed him and he served for 14 years, including as Chief Judge of the US District Court for Arizona, before my trial. His expressions did not invite questions; therefore, I didn't say anything unless directed to. My mind raced with thoughts, fear, and anxiety about my current predicament and the consequences of the actions I now faced.

Everyone talked about how President Reagan was tough on crime. He had a privatization plan that began with introducing the War on Drugs in 1982. Stricter criminal sentencing laws under Reagan led to the growth of the prison industry. He had initiated the War on Drugs to instigate a surge in mass incarcerations. He expected that would cause the prison system to collapse and open the door for the private prison industry's growth and development. Now, I faced one of his federal judicial appointees. My attorney, George Klink, asked the court for probation. He cited my cooperation with authorities, and my decision not to shave points during the fifth game as planned. He also noted my inability to play overseas that year.

The NCAA representative countered with, "One should remember that gambling on sports is not a crime without victims. The gambling is almost always backed by organized crime syndicates that launder the betting money and use it to finance drug deals, to preserve prostitution cartels, and for many other illegal activities."

The courtroom was silent as I stood before the judge. Each creak of the wood benches and the distant hum of the air conditioning were the only sounds to break the stillness. They had charged me with conspiracy to commit sports bribery, a federal crime. I was responsible for my crimes, even though others involved urged me to take part. I *felt* guilty, and the weight of my mistake, my lapse in judgment, had been heavy on my shoulders for a long time.

Naturally, I looked for a way out and a way to make amends for my wrongdoings, but the judge's cold and unyielding gaze offered no relief. I knew I had to face the consequences of my actions, whatever they may be, and I looked the judge in the eye as I accepted my fate. The courtroom was still silent as the judge tapped his gavel and spoke. "Stevin Lamarcus Smith, you are here today to answer to the charge of participating in a criminal act, and the evidence points to your involvement. How do you plead?"

Did I have a choice? Not really. My attorney and I looked at this a thousand ways and determined the best course of action was to confess my guilt. I swallowed the lump in my throat and took a deep breath before I spoke. "I plead guilty, your honor." The judge nodded, satisfied with my answer. "The court finds you guilty of conspiracy to commit sports bribery and sentences you to one year and a day in federal prison. This will be followed by three years' probation. Do you have anything to say for yourself?"

My eyes met the judge's gaze. I felt remorse for my actions. I wanted to redeem myself, not only for my sake, but for the people I had let down.

"Yes, your honor," I replied. "I want to apologize for my actions and take full responsibility for what I have done. I know I have hurt people and caused them pain, and I want to make right what I did wrong. I realize what I did was wrong. I wish I could redo it."

In my spirit, I gave my best apology, but seemingly to no avail. I am not sure what I expected, but it did not move him. "Without you, it wouldn't have happened," he said.

As the gravity of his words sank in, I looked around the courthouse. Some of the people I had betrayed, now offered me a small show of support. I was relieved, both because I had accepted my punishment and also because I was now given the opportunity to make things right. The only thing left to do was to prove myself worthy of redemption. In the spectator gallery, my mother, godmother, and girlfriend held their breaths in fragile, sorrowful silence. It devastated my mother. Upon hearing the verdict, she cried loudly and rushed out of the courtroom with Carolyn following close behind her. In contrast, DD maintained a stoic expression. She stared straight ahead, her expression unreadable. Her display of strength provided me with a sense of resilience and allowed me to depart the courtroom with my head held high, regardless of my disappointment. Of course, my father wasn't there. Not that I expected him to be, but it would have made a nice touch.

The judge's gavel boomed through the courtroom. I did not react. I had mentally prepared for this moment for months, and I steeled myself against the pain.

One figure stood still: the prosecutor. Tall and frilled in a navy-blue suit, he was the picture of justice and righteousness. As he looked out over the courtroom, I could feel his icy stare directed my way.

I dreaded this moment for so long. Life in prison was not something I had ever considered as a possibility. I thought my attorney would negotiate a lighter sentence, and I could walk away with a slap on the wrist, maybe even probation. But it was not to be. Although it could have been a lot worse. I sealed my fate by accepting justice. There was nothing else to say at the time and, along with my attorney, we declined to comment following the sentencing. Arizona State officials said nothing as well. As I prepared to serve my one year and a day in the federal bureau of prisons system, I still asked myself one question. *How did I get here?*

Rev. P. Mack, Stevin, Joe, and Brian.

Joe Gagliano and Stevin Smith share a moment after reconciliation.

CHAPTER 2: MY TESTIMONY

As you grow older, you will discover that you have two hands, one for helping yourself, the other for helping others.
—**Audrey Hepburn**

To answer the question, "How did I get here?" I had to go all the way back to my genesis, my beginning. People who are trained in psychology often ask you to go all the way back to your start to answer life's perplexing questions. "Tell me about your childhood. Tell me about your mother. Tell me about your father," they say.

Honestly, I had to do some things to uncover the genuine truth of the Stevin Hedake Smith tale that has circulated for almost 30 years. I needed to face the facts, be true to myself, and be true to God who brought me through many trials and tribulations.

Many people think they know my story. Google "Stevin Hedake Smith" and you will see 9,950,000 results. Countless others have written about me and the ASU scandal, as well as made videos and documentaries, all colored by their opinion. Truth be told, no one has heard the complete story from my point of view. Not even those closest to me, including my mother, who was my staunch supporter.

Jean-Jacques Rousseau, a Genevan philosopher writer, and composer, said something profound a long time ago. "There are always four sides to a story: your side, their side, the truth, and what really happened."

Although an important turning point in my life, the saga didn't begin with a pair of tennis shoes. I strongly believe, though, that when the afterburners turned on, they would lead me to my destiny. The shoes were white; specifically, white Jordans. Yep, those shoes. The Chicago Bulls star Michael Jordan wore the Peter Moore design in 1984 and Nike released them to the public on April 1, 1985. April Fool's Day, how ironic.

In my mind, I needed those shoes, yet my mother had a dilemma that I was not completely aware of. She had to make what could be a life-defining decision. Should she buy her baby boy basketball shoes or pay the rent? To make a long story short, she bought the white Air Jordans for $125, which resulted in our eviction because of an unpaid portion of our rent. Thankfully, Mr. Charles Thibodeaux, the apartments' custodian, used his truck to help us move our things. There was only one place we could go—MaDear's house. My mother's mom. For as long as I can remember, it was us three—a sort of Three Musketeers if you will—with the same thinking process as their motto, "All for one and one for all."

We were non-selfish like that. What one had, we all had, and it didn't stop there. In those days, neighbors willingly shared what they had with each other, even if they had little. Before we moved to Pleasant Grove, I lived in South Dallas for the first few years of my life. The borders of South Dallas included the Great Trinity Forest to the south and east; the Trinity River to the west; Interstate 30 to the north; and Downtown Dallas to the south.

South Dallas' story mirrored that of every major city in America. Jim Crow's segregation policies that discriminated against minorities in housing forged the area. People of color who tried their best to better themselves faced violence from their oppressors. South Dallas still has social and economic differences from North Dallas. However, the city of Dallas and local groups are now improving the area to attract homeowners and boost the economy.

My mama's movements were always pure, purposeful, and calculated. We moved straight from one hood to another whenever she received a raise at Southwestern Bell, the nationally known telephone company. That was the only job I knew her to have. She started out as a telephone operator and later became a forklift operator in the warehouse. That came with a huge raise, but no one cued up the theme song from television's *The Jeffersons*, "Movin' On Up."

We might not have been moving on up, however, to her credit, when we moved, it was always to a slightly better version of the previous neighborhood. Typically, it was also a better school district, although still a low-income area. For example, when we lived in South Dallas, everyone came there to get liquor. It wasn't readily available in most areas. When we moved, it was across the bridge to Pleasant Grove, maybe a smidgen better than the area we left. She wanted nothing but the best for her only child, Stevin Lamarcus Smith, a.k.a Hedake. By the way, I'm always asked, "How did you get the name, Hedake?"

The story is funny, but you needed to hear my mother tell it to get the full gist of it. When I was born at Dallas Osteopathic Hospital on January 23, 1972, I weighed seven pounds and one and a half ounces. According to my mother, 95 percent of that was my head. Early childhood photos seem to bear that out.

I was a boisterous young boy, and as a single mother, she sometimes found me to be troublesome, although I didn't get into real trouble. I was a busybody. Apparently, God gave me tons of energy and I could play all day long. The old folks called it being a "handful" but I was a headache. As a result, she started calling me "Headache," which became an adoring little nickname she used only for me. How one spells my name is a completely different matter.

When I was five or six years old, Mama wanted to get individualized license plates for her brand-new, burgundy-colored, Buick Regal. She wasn't a stranger to hard work, and she rewarded herself for her diligence. She bought it with her own sweat, blood, and tears, and wanted to put customized plates on it. The DMV limited personalized plates to six characters, so Headache wasn't an option. Using her creativity, she came up with "Hedake." Mama has always been good at thinking on her feet. She had to be because society tasked her with raising a young black man in the hood as a single parent.

Speaking of the day I was born; I am the only person I know with two legitimate birthdays. My arrival occurred on January 24, 1972, at 6:58 p.m., although the doctor's initial prediction pronounced I would make my grand entrance into the world on January 25. However, for reasons we still cannot comprehend, both my birth certificate and driver's license show January 23, 1972. I have always enjoyed treating myself to some of my favorite items on both days, like baked fish, Tito's vodka, and a meal at Pappadeaux Seafood Kitchen.

By design, I am the only child of my mother. Notwithstanding the joy and significance of my birth, it was also traumatic for her. Because of the trauma and drama surrounding my birth, she had her tubes tied shortly afterward. She led me to believe it was health-related and chances are I would never have given it another thought. Many black women have difficulty in childbirth, although society depicts otherwise. Researchers are studying the alarming maternal mortality rates in the United States. Black mothers in the US have a death rate three to four times higher than white mothers, the largest health disparity among all races. To put it another way, a black woman has a 24% higher risk of dying from causes related to pregnancy or childbirth. According to a national study, "Black women were two to three times more likely than white women who had the same condition to die of five medical complications that are common causes of maternal death and injury."

As a child, I don't think I fully understood, except for the occasional longing for a little brother. It didn't bother me to be an only child. It was only after I was much older that I realized how difficult childbirth can be. To remind her of that, my mother put a bumper sticker on her car. The sticker read, "The Bigger the Headache the Bigger the Pill," a popular song by George Clinton and Parliament-Funkadelic.

The sticker and her customized license plates were funny and gave my mom the opportunity to pay tribute to me at the same time. With a mom like that, I'm not sure I would have been willing to share her with any siblings, anyway. When MaDear wasn't around, we were a "dynamic duo" much like Batman and Robin. Life was full, and to be completely honest, I didn't miss the father I never knew. Being raised by a single mother in the black community was common, so I thought little about him. But from time to time, he ran across my mind.

Sociologists have claimed that two-parent families improve children's health, education, and finances. This might be true, but sometimes you have to play the hand dealt to you in the face of adversity. What else could anyone do?

A report from 2016 found that over one-third of black children under 18 in the US live with unmarried mothers, compared to only 6.5% of white children. With an intimate knowledge of the situation, I can say with authority, most black women in this circumstance, kick it up a notch or two. They do everything they can to make up for the absence of the father. I won't parrot what I have heard many say, that they are the child's or children's mother and father. I will say my mother pulled out all the stops to make sure I didn't lack anything. Yet, there was always a foreboding feeling that "not enough" was right around the corner.

Anyway, my upbringing seemed normal and when I was six years old, I discovered basketball. It became my first love. I was a typical black child growing up in a hood without a father, structure, or weekends spent at Chuck-E-Cheese. My mother was in recovery mode when she wasn't working at Southwestern Bell, which employed her for 28 years before she retired. When her doctor diagnosed her with colon cancer, her employer forced her to retire in 1994. Yet, she attempted to enjoy every waking moment when she wasn't working.

My closest friends were my cousins; Shun, Keith, Cortez, Norron, and Norris. We grew up more like siblings, so to speak. When we weren't at school, we were in the streets. The heat in Texas is real, as anyone who has visited the state knows. Yet, as children, we couldn't have cared less. Occasionally, my cousins and I would play from dusk to dawn until we were too hot or too starved to continue. In "Sunny South Dallas," we spent our days playing basketball on the outdoor courts at Charles Rice Elementary, eating sandwiches and oatmeal cakes. Afterward, we spent most of the evenings at MaDear's house, and did homework at her kitchen table until dinner.

My mother felt I was a natural at basketball and she decided it was time to take my street ball to the next level after school. She enrolled me in the basketball program at the Park South

YMCA. The Young Men Christian Association or YMCA as we know it, lived up to its motto: "To put Christian values into practice through programs that build a healthy spirit, mind, and body for all." That kept me occupied until I experienced Biddy Basketball, which was regarded as the genuine thing. Biddy Basketball taught boys and girls the fundamentals and skills of the game. The organization made the sport more competitive for younger players by using shorter goals, a smaller ball, and height restrictions.

In 1981, at nine years old, I became a Pleasant Grove Trojan, or "that green and gold outta' that greedy grove," as we used to say, and my life changed forever. That's when the name "Hedake" first became notable on the court. It was no longer a pet name between my mother and me. Some players chose names like The Admiral, King, Mailman, and Magic. All of those were illustrious names, but I didn't want to be like Mike. I was an original, and I was a headache for anyone who tried to guard me. Carl Richardson Sr. helped me develop skills, temperament, and determination that served me well in football, basketball, baseball, and life.

My cousin, Coach Wade Taylor II, provided me with additional guidance during all seasons of every sport I played. We were family, and he saw my potential. Playing with the Trojans from elementary school through junior high school changed my life, without a doubt. It was a privilege for me to play basketball, baseball, and football. I was a triple threat because I was good at both football and baseball, but I was special at basketball. I gave up the other two sports after the ninth grade to concentrate solely on basketball.

For a long time, all I knew about Nathel Green, my father, was that he lived in Highland Hills, around the corner from my mother's aunt—my great aunt—Aunt Leola. She was the sister of my mother's dad. Aunt Leola stood about six foot one. She had seven children: three girls and four boys. I called her my gangster aunt. She didn't play. But she went to church every Sunday and her heart was as big as they come. Just don't cross her. If it were not for her, my mother would not have had any free time. Since she worked so much trying to provide for me, Aunt Leola would often make it possible for my mother to have some recreation time in her life. She would keep me and that allowed my mother time for rest and recuperation. I also spent most of my summers at her house.

My father wasn't a part of my life. It was as if he didn't exist. Or maybe to him, it was the other way around; I didn't exist. When I asked my mother about it, she said, "He has a whole other life, baby."

Even at such a young age, I knew she resented talking about him, though she never explicitly criticized him. That in itself was a life lesson for me. As a result, I didn't ask too many questions. I didn't realize how she really felt about him until much later. Eventually, I found out why her pride prevented her from asking him for money and why his name wasn't on my birth certificate. Additionally, she never compelled him to pay child support. Aunt Leola tried to get my mother to put my father "on child support," but she refused. My mother felt she shouldn't have to beg a man to take care of his own son.

After a chance encounter at the barbershop when I was nine years old, the question mark surrounding my father became less of a mystery. Occasionally, even though money was tight, Mama would find a way to take me to Mr. Bouie's Barber Shop in Pleasant Grove. It was nothing fancy, certainly not part of any national franchise. Yet, the men who made their way to Mr. Bouie's in the early 80s, felt, in the words of Rev. Jesse Jackson, "I am somebody!"

Somehow, I knew there was something special about the neighborhood barbershop, although I couldn't quite put my finger on it. Traditionally, barbershops have been more than a place to get a haircut. They are a social gathering place for men. Many men visited on a weekly basis, like some type of ritual. There they would wait for their turn, to either get a shave or a haircut. But that's not all they were doing. Though men joke about avoiding women, they also went to barbershops to socialize, relax, and bond with others who had similar interests. Whenever my mother took me, there would be regulars. Some, you would think, had nothing else to do because they were always there. They were never in a hurry to leave, even after the barbers had provided the service. I can't vouch for the level of conversation before I arrived, but whenever my mother or any other female showed up, the talk was always respectful.

Anyway, on this day, I was there by myself. I waited my turn to get a haircut and a strange feeling came over me. You know how it feels when someone is staring at you, but you are afraid to look because they might catch you looking back? The man who stared at me was my father, Nathel Green, also known as Scooner. I resembled him in every way. He had large hands and an enormous head like mine, but he was short and pigeon-toed.

"Hello, Hedake!" he finally said from the barber's chair across the room. "It's me, Scooner."

He said it like I was supposed to know who he was, with a mix of confidence and arrogance. Yes, I knew *of* him, but I didn't *know* him. On that day in that barbershop, time stood still. This was a meeting that was almost 10 years in the making. *How should I act? What should I do? What should I say?*

I had never seen him eye-to-eye up to that point, yet I had often heard his name. Sometimes I heard the name whispered from behind Mama's bedroom doors or casually discussed in MaDear's kitchen. There's not much else I remember about the encounter or how I felt about seeing him.

He said, "Say hello to your mother."

He then reached into his pocket and gave me a few dollars. Wow! Almost ten years and he gave me a dollar for each year. I didn't know if I should be thankful or not even take the cash. Of course, I did.

When I got home, I couldn't wait to tell Mama I had met my father. I yelled, "Mama, I met Scooner!" before I even inserted my key into the apartment lock. When it came to anything that was related to my father and her, she didn't say a word, but that was typical. I'm not sure what I had expected. *Perhaps in my mind, she would say something like, That's good, baby! Then I could tell her about the money he gave me and all would be right in the world. The next thing I knew, as a family, we would get ice cream cones at the State Fair of Texas.* If that was my dream, her stony silence awakened me.

As a child I was unaware of the complexity of male-female relationships. I didn't know how difficult it was to have a child with a man who didn't promise a relationship or a long-term commitment. As a young black boy who grew up quickly to be a young black man, I couldn't understand why Mama kept everything about my father a secret. In fact, I didn't realize how shameful and stigmatizing my mother's actions were until much later.

She could not admit her error because of her pride, so she really didn't talk about the specifics of their relationship with me. I know my mother was firm; some people say she had an attitude. To me, she was serious. When I became a little older, I joked with her and said, "Mama, you will snap in a minute." Of course, I kept my distance when I said that. She was protective of herself and of me. I didn't think that would ever change.

Once, I said, "Mom, slow down. You are too aggressive with me!" And at that time, I was a grown man with my own daughters.

Honestly, I was confused. I wasn't mad at my father. I never comprehended how or why he couldn't or didn't have any desire to be in his own child's life. One thing I know is that when you make the mistake of going back and digging, you learn enough to know. Later, I found out my father had 12 other children, one of whom had died. Even though I cannot pinpoint a single incident that sparked my desire to forge a relationship with him, there is one episode that stands out. And this brings me back to the occasion concerning the white Jordans.

One day when I got home from school, I noticed someone had lined up all our belongings and laid them out on the sidewalk. It was like we were having a garage sale. I didn't know what an eviction was and probably couldn't even spell it, much less comprehend the scope of what transpired that day. Mama didn't pay her rent the month before, as I later discovered. *How did this come about?* I pondered. Especially considering I knew Mama worked every day and always seemed to have a man around to ease the load. Certainly, that was my assumption.

In her narrative, Mama asked my father for help with the shoes because money was tight, but he turned her down. They weren't for style, neither were they a luxury. I needed a good pair of basketball shoes because I now took the sport seriously. Knowing my Mama, she struggled to swallow her pride and ask Scooner for money. Her only solution was to make a sacrifice. And sacrifice she did. She didn't pay rent in order to give her son the pair of basketball shoes he desperately needed. More than the price on the tag, it cost us our apartment.

MaDear graciously let us move in with her. I will always be grateful to God for our praying and loving grandmother. She did her best to raise me right without a male figure, along with Mama. I don't include the roughly twenty "step-daddies" who entered and left my life throughout elementary and high school. I'm not exaggerating. My mother was a "thick Foxy Brown," type with a cute face and shoulder-length brown hair. Many men wanted her on their arm, but you had to come correct or get to stepping. That's probably why I don't remember all their names or faces.

Only a few of them stuck in my mind, and none of them were likely to have the same impact on my life as my father would. On our coffee table were photos of her with three men. I did not know who they were. To me, they were the man with the dark glasses, the man with the perm, and the man with all the rings on his fingers. When I got older and listened to secular music, I had several "I'll be…" moments. They turned out to be Ray Charles, James Brown, and Johnnie Taylor. The only one I met, though, was Johnnie Taylor because he was from Dallas. One day, my mother took me to his office off Highway 35 by the zoo in Oak Cliff. They were good friends and while they visited, I looked around the office and the photos, awards, and accolades on the walls amazed me.

Some of the other men in my life would occasionally give me a few dollars. However, none of them ever took the time to get to know me or taught me any values about being a man, or a productive member of society. That came from within. I knew I had to be a different father to my children when I considered the shoes, rent, and other interactions concerning Scooner. By the way, my father did not respond to my birthdays, Christmases, or even the moves over the years. Whatever life had in store for me, I had to break the cycle.

Stevin (standing), spending time with his cousins, Shun, Cortez, and Keith.

Stevin left, and his cousin, Keith.

Stevin Smith and his father, Nathel Green, aka, Scooner.

CHAPTER 3: HE SAW THE BEST IN ME

*Every child is an artist. The problem is how
to remain an artist when we grow up.*
–Pablo Picasso

In the iconic movie *Mama, I Want to Sing!* the storyline follows a talented young singer on the brink of fame. After her father's sudden death, her mother steps into the role of preacher, ascending to the top of the gospel world. Simultaneously, the young singer becomes a massive R&B sensation. However, tension arises when the mother disapproves of the daughter's secular music. The young singer must balance her aspirations with the challenges of fame, while staying true to herself and her family. If this movie was about my life, I would probably title it, *Mama, I Want to Play Basketball!*

As a young child, I hadn't heard the renowned story of how James Naismith invented the game of basketball. Eventually, I learned how he created a new indoor game for college students to play during the long New England winters. His invention would play an indelible impact on my life.

I spent my adolescence oscillating between an intense focus on basketball and seeking guidance from my dedicated coach, who played the part of a somewhat proxy father. Apart from a notable relocation, the summer before middle school was relatively uneventful. By relocating, my mother felt it would give me a better opportunity. Texas implemented the "No Pass, No Play" policy in 1984. Public school students needed to maintain a minimum GPA to take part in extracurricular activities. The law applied to all grades for activities outside of class, including UIL activities. If a student failed one class, they were ineligible for those activities. Unfortunately, because of my poor academic performance throughout middle school, I couldn't participate in sports at E.B. Comstock Middle School.

Rather than being defined by the setback, I improved my skills and played for the Trojans with the help of Coach Richardson and Coach Taylor, who guided me throughout my middle school years. Not that I wasn't smart; I was in a different mental place. To make it plain, I was a knucklehead. I don't blame others, but this was definitely a case of hanging around the wrong people.

Much is to be said about peer pressure. According to raisingchildren.net.au, "Peer influence is when you choose to do something you wouldn't otherwise do, because you want to feel accepted and valued by your friends. It isn't just or always about doing something against your will." Since my lot was cast, I would have to make do with my negative choices.

Middle school—seventh and eighth grades—would be over in a couple of years. I would then be on to high school with its own challenges. The basketball court served as a significant part of my life and left little time for me to ponder the absence of my father. Like many others, I attempted to suppress the impact of this trauma, seemingly unaffected by it. Only later, did I comprehend how profoundly it influenced my lifestyle and the way I cherished my family.

In the movies, the focus of a coming-of-age narrative is typically on the emotional and ethical development of the main character as they transition from youth to adulthood. The writer places significant emphasis in this type of story on character evolution. Like many high school athletes, a pivotal moment in my life occurred when I entered high school. Most young boys can't wait to drive, get a job, their first real girlfriend, etc. I was no different. The emphasis on my life plan was to excel in basketball and use high school to win a college scholarship and then launch a career in the NBA.

I couldn't wait to get to H. Grady Spruce High School. Most students go to particular schools because they are in their community, without giving thought to the person the school is named after. The label that a school building carries can hold substantial significance. Many educational institutions cherish their names, allocating considerable time and energy to recount the history behind their names on their online platforms. The presence of school names is conspicuous on sports grounds, educational resources, stickers, and apparel.

In recent years, protesters have made a push to change the names of schools that reflect Confederate identities and/or names of schools that held monikers of former slave owners. According to research conducted by Education Week, around 340 schools across 21 states and the District of Columbia presently carry the names of Confederate figures. From June 29, 2020, at least 60 schools named after Confederate leaders have changed their names, with Texas and Virginia housing 35 of these institutions.

H. Grady Spruce High School has a proud legacy. The "H" stands for Henry. The school is named after Henry Grady Spruce, a Texas native from Omen, an unincorporated area in Smith County. Spruce held degrees from both Southern Methodist University, as well as, the University of Chicago. He dedicated a substantial part of his 35-year career with the YMCA to the youth, serving as the director of the Dallas

YMCA's Camp Crockett (now known as Camp Grady Spruce) near Granbury and the Park Cities YMCA for 25 years. The YMCA of Metropolitan Dallas started its camp programs in 1922 at Camp Crockett. During World War II, they moved it to Dallas on Bachman Lake at Camp Kiwanis.

In 1949, Eugene Constantin donated his land on Possum Kingdom Lake to the YMCA in memory of his son who died in service, marking the first summer camp there. They named the camp after H. Grady Spruce, a respected YMCA Youth Secretary. The late 1950s saw an increased demand for boys camping at Camp Grady Spruce, which led to the opening of the Frontier Camp in 1960. Girls started attending the camp in the 1960s and by 1973, the Ray Bean camp for girls and families was established. In 1983, the Frontier Camp became a co-ed program.

Once an integral part of Rylie, Dallas incorporated the territory in the late 1950s and it evolved into a community primarily recognized for its high school, H. Grady Spruce, established in 1963. This school took the place of Rylie High School, which was transformed into a junior high school and subsequently a middle school in 1972. Upon its inauguration, Spruce's student population mirrored the local community and was majority white, with some black students and representatives from other ethnic groups. Starting in 1971, Spruce participated in busing. The shift in the demographics of the Pleasant Grove area in the early 1980s led to black students becoming the majority. In the 1990s, Hispanics emerged as the majority group. In 1963, Spruce High School adopted the "Mighty Fighting Apaches" as their mascot. However, in 1998, the school changed its mascot to the Timberwolves.

When I entered high school in 1987, I encountered the legendary Coach Val Rhodes, up close and personal. It is difficult to overstate the impact of Coach Rhodes, as his status extends well beyond sports. We created long-lasting bonds that went beyond sports by valuing connections and staying focused on improvement.

Thirty-seven years later, Coach Rhodes is rounding out his 47th year in education. He recently served as interim principal at Texas Can Oak Cliff. After the administrators hired a new principal, Coach Rhodes focused on his two businesses. He owns the Coach Val Rhodes Youth foundation, which helps empower youth with life skills and behavior ethics, and Rhodes Educational Network LLC, a research-based consulting business.

In the words of Coach Rhodes

I first noticed Stevin when he was in the 8th grade. I came to Spruce around 1984 and he came there later as a freshman. But there was a Trojan program in the area that many of the children from H. Grady Spruce were a part of, led by Coach Carl Richardson. Stevin and Carl Richardson Jr., the coach's son, were buddies. I saw them play and realized how talented they were. I knew that once they made it to high school, they would be stars.

When I first saw them on the court, they were playing with eight-foot goals, then they moved up to the regulation 10-foot goals. The freshman team led by one of my football coaches, was outstanding. In his sophomore year, Stevin played for me on the varsity squad; I brought him off the bench. Previously, he didn't have a reputation as an outside shooter. Stevin was a driver; he headed to the bucket, dished the ball and so forth, but over the summer he worked on his three-point shooting. He started shooting many threes in his sophomore year and he was on fire from three-point range most of the time. I had an outstanding point guard, Leslie Booker, a senior who went on to play for New Mexico Junior College. When Stevin played during his junior year, he took over the position and we had an excellent team for the next two years.

Besides his raw talents and gifts, what stood out about Stevin was his infectious nature around people. Everybody, including all the older guys, looked at him and knew he was going to be good and they all had positive opinions about him. He took over the team through his leadership ability—something else that caused everyone to love him. You could see that love when he walked down the campus' hallways. Doors would open and students would yell out, "Hedake! Hedake!"

Even today, when I meet former coaches whom I coached against, the first thing they ask is, "How is Hedake doing?" and "Have you heard from him?" His name and my name became synonymous with one another. But it's not only in the Spruce area; he also has a great following everywhere, including on social media. People ask about him all over. At a younger age, he was so well-liked, he would often be in the company of Larry Johnson, an all American at UNLV or Spud Webb and guys like that. The summer league had just opened up for the youth in Texas. In his senior year, we put him in a five-star camp in Pittsburg. Evidently, he shined at camp and when he got back, I received more calls from people wanting to come in and see him from Jerry Tarkanian of UNLV to John Thompson of Georgetown.

He narrowed his choices down and he happened to meet the new coach from Cincinnati, Ohio. He wanted to let him come on a home visit, and Texas also did a home visit, but as far as where he really wanted to go, I didn't know. When he got back from visiting Arizona State, he was excited. He had one more visit left, and that was to Arizona University.

I suggested, "Stevin, you know Arizona University has a better program."

He said, "I know, Coach. But I think I want to go to Arizona State." I didn't think much about it. I had built a great relationship with the assistant coach, George McQuarn, and I felt comfortable with him.

When the point-shaving scandal came to light, I knew nothing about it. Before the draft, I received several phone calls from a few NBA teams asking about him, but no one said anything. I gave them the positive things I knew about him and that was that. And even on NBA draft night, when no one took him, I wasn't worried about it. I knew if someone would give him a chance, he would be fine. He eventually joined the CBA (Continental Basketball Association) where he waited for the NBA opportunity.

A while later, I received a call. "Judge!" the voice on the other end stated. Coach Alex Gillman who used to be at Carter High School called all the players "Judge" and I started doing that as well. When I heard that, I knew it was him. He continued, "Can you come to the game today?"

"What game?"

"The Mavericks."

"What do you mean?"

"I signed a 10-day contract with the Mavericks."

"Yeah, I'll be there." I had been working for the Mavericks with their summer camps. I called somebody and got some tickets and walked into the arena. Stevin was over on the bench.

"Hey, here! Hey, here!" I said.

It was a phrase I always used. He immediately looked up, with that smile of his, and I watched them play. He also got into the game. I was proud of him. This is what he always wanted and what many of us saw for him.

He came back into town and I didn't know. When he came to see me, I had my back to the door, and I was on the north end of the gym. I heard the door open behind me; the team kept playing. However, they weren't playing the way they used to. They all increased their game. I thought, *okay, something just happened*. Then I turned around, and I saw Stevin. He was over in a corner.

"Hey, baby boy. What's going on?" I asked.

He came over and gave me a hug. He didn't say much.

"Coach, you always taught me to do the right thing. I love you and I appreciate you and whatever happens, I want you to know I love you."

"Sure. No problem. I love you, too."

We hugged and he left. We finished practice. When I got home, I sat down to watch television and suddenly the news broke on ESPN. They showed a photo of Stevin playing overseas and flashed other information. Then they talked about what happened at Arizona State University.

The scandal didn't change anything in my mind because he was my son. I treated the situation as a son who made a mistake, and that was that. Remember, he's from Pleasant Grove. He wasn't supposed to be where he's at. He wasn't supposed to make it in the pros. Maybe he wasn't even supposed to go to college.

You couldn't look at his games at ASU and tell something was going on because he always went out to be the best possible player. No, the mistake he made didn't change us. As a matter of fact, our bond became tighter. I will always love him. He's a great person with a great heart. One thing that goes bad, does not or should not define a person. Bad things happen to good people. There are people all over this nation, all over this world, who had something that didn't go right. Yet, they had the ability to change and make the best out of it. That's why years later, we are still in touch with each other. When the organizers honored me with The Gordon Wood Hall of Champions Induction Ceremony about four hours from here in West Texas, he made an appearance. And, standing with me and my family, he took photos with us because he *is* part of our family. It has always been like that.

It's amazing, though, how the NCAA wanted to throw the book at him. They wanted to make an example out of him. And now, he's flying out across the nation as a speaker, because he is an example. Stevin has been beneficial in helping young people stay on the right track and be lovable. He was a lovable young boy, and now he's such a lovable young man. He's an overcomer.

Do I wish he could not have been in that situation and didn't go through everything he went through? Do I wonder what life would have been for him had he had a long professional basketball career?

Yes, for sure, but the bottom line is he took a lemon and made lemonade out of it. He's living his life and he's loving family life. I think something more positive will come out of him. Something big will happen down the road. A great blessing is in store for the one we call, "Hedake."

******

As a freshman, attending Spruce was probably the most excited I've ever been because it was a new beginning. It was a seminal moment. Finally, I was in high school and it excited me to no end. I also played tight end in football. As a tight end, I was above average because I could catch pretty good. I knew it would be tough for me to play varsity basketball as a freshman because the team overflowed with talented basketball players. However, going to Spruce helped pave the way because I learned a lot. One lesson I learned was how to have patience. For example, Leslie Booker was in front of me. However, he too, had to wait for his time because there was somebody in front of him. Plus, the varsity players had too much pride to let freshmen come in and take their spots. For me, it was a process. Many people have said, "I played on varsity as a freshman." But I couldn't say that; I had to wait for my turn.

Coach Rhodes was pretty hard on me. Over the four years, we developed a great relationship, but it took time because I had to build trust with him. He had to trust me. I found out it was the same thing with Leslie. It's that way with all great point guards. Trust must develop between the player and coach. At Comstock I wasn't eligible, but at Spruce, I was always eligible. That was a big step forward. Everyone looked at me as being just another freshman among many good freshmen. As a testament to his prowess, Coach Rhodes' training paved the way for many of his players to take part in Division I sports, the NFL, and the NBA. He attributed his coaching skills to his time learning from great basketball mentors. That included Coach Robert Hughes Sr., the "all-time winningest high school basketball coach in America," and hall of famer, Coach J.D. Mayo,.

From the moment I held a basketball at the age of five, to when I saw my first game on television, I knew the NBA was my destiny. However, with each passing year, I also understood that this dream was not easily attainable. To play alongside the best, one had to become the best. My mother's strong work ethic, a value she ingrained within me, served as an excellent example.

She often reminded me, "If you don't work, you don't eat." Later, I discovered this principle in the Bible in 2 Thessalonians 3:10. This simple yet powerful statement fueled my motivation to excel in the sport of basketball. It would be difficult to find anyone who worked harder than I did on the court, from my early days in grade school all the way until my career ended in 2008. Although a natural-born disciplinarian, Coach Rhodes was notably stricter with me than others. He was hard on me at first; I didn't think he liked me. I eventually realized it was a mental thing. He wanted to see how tough I was. However, the times I wanted to break down in tears or escape to a hidden corner, I did my utmost to maintain a stoic demeanor.

Years later, he explained that his tough approach was necessary for my progress. He said, "You would've never taken it seriously, Hed, if I hadn't been so hard. I was preparing you not just for college, but for something much bigger. You don't take anything seriously until they take away something from you."

Eventually, my actions had consequences that caused me to lose my dignity, privacy, and NBA dreams. Let me take you through the days when things seemed promising before my activities snatched away those dreams. Our freshman team only lost one game throughout the season. This powerful performance provided me with valuable experience and prepared me for greater opportunities.

As a sophomore, I moved up to the varsity team and received substantial playing time. My peers recognized my skills, and it earned me the title of "Sophomore of the Year." My progress accelerated as I entered my junior year, which marked a turning point in my career.

I was fortunate to become the starting point guard when Leslie Booker graduated. Along with All-American shooting guard, Isaac Williams (Ike Moe), we made a formidable duo on the court. Ike Moe was a young star with nationwide attention; his presence attracted college recruiters and allowed me to be discovered. I owe much of my early success to him because he played a significant role in shaping my path.

Another lesson I learned throughout this journey was the importance of discipline and determination, both on and off the court. Unlike my middle school days, I maintained good grades and avoided disciplinary issues for a short period. My time under Coach Rhodes transformed me not only into a better athlete, but also a more dedicated student and a better person overall. At Spruce, I rapidly gained popularity and a reputation for being an up-and-coming basketball star. My popularity extended to social circles. However, my journey was not without its difficulties. Academic performance and behavior were two areas where I faced challenges. Coach Rhodes kept a watchful eye on me and was eager to address any issue I encountered.

One notable challenge was the preparation for my first SAT test. Ms. Betty Brown, a high school counselor, and Karen Butler, my math teacher, took it upon themselves to support me. Ms. Brown ensured I received all the necessary tools for success, from study materials to instructional videos. Initially, I failed the test, yet, I triumphantly aced my second one, and earned a remarkable score that attracted the NCAA's attention. This was my first interaction with the NCAA but I had no idea it would not be my last.

The authorities at the NCAA questioned my improved scores, but Ms. Brown stood her ground. She wrote a letter to the NCAA explaining her teaching methods and defending my accomplishments. Similarly, Coach Rhodes was an unwavering pillar of support, both on and off the court. His tough attitude made me strong enough to handle any challenges.

Throughout my high school basketball journey, Coach Rhodes' guidance was invaluable. He stepped up and showed me how to be a man. To a great degree, he was a father to me. Although I had met my father, he was not active in my life. Like a father figure, he supported me both on and off the court. I couldn't put my finger on it, but now I know mentorship and father-figures are essential to young inner-city children. This is particularly true for black males.

Mentors and father-figures provide positive role models in environments often marked by negative influences. These figures help with life's challenges, like school problems and peer pressure. They foster increased self-esteem and confidence by believing in these youths' potential. In addition, they also encourage them not to let their circumstances limit their futures. Studies have linked mentorship to reduced engagement in risky behaviors and improved academic success.

A father-figure who understands the experiences of black males can provide valuable emotional support. This is especially true when dealing with racism and bias. Therefore, the role of mentorship and father-figures is crucial in shaping the lives of young inner-city kids, especially black males.

One thing Coach Rhodes taught me to master was to never break down in a heated situation. And he didn't only mean this in basketball; he meant in life. That message was bigger than a game. Little did I know that at the moment. But there's one thing we always did as a team. Before and after every game, we would come together in a circle and hold hands as he prayed. He led every prayer. I remember the words like it was yesterday and I say them to this day. "Most gracious, heavenly Father, we come to you as humble as we know." I knew the words he said, but after I got older, I understood what he said and the value of prayer. Like most of us, I had learned "The Lord's Prayer" or "The Model Prayer," but he sincerely prayed for us each time we went out on the court. Win, lose, or draw, that's what he did. And he didn't do it for a show; he is a godly man and a faithful Christian. He prayed out of dedication, to his career, his team, his God, and his church, Concord Church in Dallas, where he serves as a deacon. And that was one of the life lessons I learned from him. Pray without ceasing.

As time went on, I became better and contributed much to our continued success. During my junior year, our team flourished. We reached the Regionals and made significant strides. However, we fell short, losing in the fourth round to Humble High School, which won the state championship that year. While we lost, my passion for the sport remained unwavering.

I also excelled in tournaments sponsored by Coca-Cola, Dr. Pepper, and Grapevine, that was open to all high schools. My success in basketball was due to both my three-point shooting skills and my ability to remain calm under pressure. Coach Rhodes recognized that as being crucial. This resilience and determination set me apart from my fellow teammates, as I refused to back down from challenges or adversaries.

As my junior year ended, organizers chose me as one of the top 12 players in the Dallas-Fort Worth region for my AAU team, Dallas Metro Allstars. We were all invited to the Las Vegas Invitational. There were 250 teams in the tournament and our team emerged victorious. Due to my performance, I was named Co-MVP.

I will never forget that experience because all the top coaches in the country were present, and the public packed the stands. The goal of coaches in the Amateur Athletic Association (AAU) is to get their players noticed by the recruiters that represent the various colleges and universities. I went three times; as a freshman, a sophomore, and a junior. Mind you, every team does not make it to the big stage, but we made it during my junior year. The first two years were still exciting because we were in Las Vegas and whenever we could, we would watch the older guys play. They filled the tournament with talented basketball players and the rest of us dreamed about being on the big stage. The number of scouts that showed up also amazed us.

At that time, there was only one big tournament. It is still one of the largest. Now you have the Nike, Adidas, Reebok, New Balance, and Under Armour Tournaments. We could barely wait for our opportunity. When we got our chance, we didn't disappoint anyone. ESPN broadcast the championship game held at the Thomas and Mack Center at the University of Las Vegas.

Of course, people said, "What happens in Vegas, stays in Vegas," but that's not true in this case, or wanted. In 1989, people didn't highly recognize Texas high school basketball. We had a chance to gain respect for our state across the country. The competition was top-notch. It consisted of all the top players from across the country. My strategy was simple: "All it takes is all you got. If you don't give all you got, you don't have what it takes." That was my mentality and how I prepared for the tournament. That is also my advice to young players coming up. Give it your all on the court. You will have ups and downs for sure, but when you leave the court, make sure you gave it your all. Don't leave anything behind.

For me, being at the tournament was a dream come true; the first rung of the ladder to becoming a star basketball player. Personally, I averaged 18 points, five rebounds, five assists and three steals. We didn't only represent DFW; we represented the state of Texas. We were the first team from Texas to win it and people still talk about it. That game put me on the map and gave me nationwide attention. I can't even count the number of phone calls and letters I received from interested parties after that win. Not only was I on the first team from Texas to win it but to be named Co-MVP, you can't buy that type of recognition. Being selected as Co-MVP was a true blessing. It wasn't my beginning, but it was the genesis of my understanding of Philippians 4:13: "I can do all things through Christ which strengtheneth me."

Ed O'Bannon Jr. was the other Co-MVP of the tournament, although our teams never played each other. He attended Bishop Gorman High School in Las Vegas. He also made a commitment to UNLV but attended UCLA when the school was placed on probation for infractions. We played against each other eight times over the next four years, and I never won against him. He was a power forward for the Bruins on their 1995 NCAA championship team. The New Jersey Nets selected him with the ninth overall pick of the 1995 NBA draft.

After the Invitational, I attended the prestigious Five-Star basketball camp in Pittsburg, where I played alongside the top 100 players in the nation. This week-long event concluded with me being acknowledged as one of the elite point guards in attendance. Following this recognition, the attention and interest of major schools intensified.

It's ironic that Las Vegas is where I first gained notoriety. It's also home to the first university I committed to, UNLV. However, years later, the city earned notoriety as the site where millions of dollars illegally flowed in what was perhaps the biggest gambling scandal at the time.

Coach Val Rhodes was instrumental in developing Stevin as a top notch basketball player.

The Dallas Metro Allstars, (AAU Team).

Stevin and Carl Richardson Jr.

CHAPTER 4: NEW THING

We can only learn to love by loving.

—Iris Murdoch

Throughout my senior year, I remained diligent and focused on completing the season with outstanding results. Bright futures awaited both Carl Jr. and me. A multitude of universities offered us full scholarships, with him excelling in football and me in basketball. As highly regarded athletes, we had an undeniable charm that attracted attention in our school and beyond.

On the evening of our senior prom, we left no stone unturned for making it an unforgettable night. We coordinated our attire with matching tuxedos and invited two exquisite young ladies to accompany us. To elevate the experience, we rented two 1989 Nissan Maximas. Carl Jr. and I celebrated our success and enjoyed a moment of triumph.

However, an unexpected event nearly jeopardized our prom attendance. Dr. Childs, our assistant principal, caught Marlon Bass, Fet Taylor, Lil' Lamont, Rod Taylor, Carl Jr., Perry Wilborn and me, gambling in a dimly lit corner of the gymnasium after seventh period. After he discovered our misbehavior, he summoned us to his office the following day. We faced harsh repercussions, including the possibility of being banned from the prom. However, Coach Rhodes' intervention spared us from severe punishment, and they gave us in-school detention. Early on, friends and friends of family members, exposed me to the world of gambling and I learned how to navigate it.

At eleven, my neighbor, Tony Turner, introduced me to the game of dice. He believed I needed to gain the knowledge to earn money quickly rather than solely relying on my mother to provide for all my needs. Tony pointed out that since my mother was already facing financial hardships, it was important for me to find an alternative way to help support our family.

Though my mother was well aware of my occasional participation in gambling, she chose not to discipline me for it. It could have been because she had a habit of engaging with lotteries and playing football squares during football season, both of which involved taking minor risks. Basketball, though, was not a gamble. Having cast my lot with UNLV, as a young teenager, I walked the halls of Spruce High School adorned in the university's apparel. My decision to join the Rebels was a wrap, and my presence prompted whispers, stares, and undeniable curiosity from my peers. They soon understood that I was determined to join the ranks of UNLV, and pursue my academic and athletic aspirations.

As the popular saying goes, "If you want to make God laugh, tell Him about your plans." Choosing a college for basketball seemed set in stone; I was on the verge of committing to the University of Nevada, Las Vegas. However, as fate would have it, we had to pause our decision as the university faced NCAA probation charges related to illegal recruiting. UNLV received a ban from televised games and post-season competition for the 1991-92 season. Fortunately, Arizona State University (ASU) remained a viable alternative. Coach Rhodes had a good relationship with Coach George McQuarn, and he facilitated communications between the two parties. After I talked to the coaches, they watched me play a couple of times in Dallas.

Before my trip to the university, a lavish surprise arrived at my doorstep: a limousine organized by Roy Tarpley, a player for the Dallas Mavericks. He intended to provide me with a memorable experience, complete with courtside seats at a game, to endorse his former coach at Michigan, Bill Frieder, who was now at ASU.

Upon my visit to the campus, several similarities struck me as compared to my previous visit to Las Vegas. A professionally dressed representative welcomed me at the airport and escorted me to a hotel, where I met some of the current players. While the setting may not have been as luxurious as what I experienced in Vegas, it still offered an impressive introduction to college life.

I had the pleasure of staying at the South Mountain Resort—one of the most luxurious hotels in the region. My host for the duration of my stay was Terrance Wheeler, a junior player on the college basketball team. Wheeler, or "T-Wheeler" as I fondly called him, hailed from Detroit, and quickly became one of my closest friends on the team. Our friendship endured the test of time.

When I met Coach Frieder for the first time, his relatively short stature struck me. Although he visited Dallas earlier in the year, accompanied by one of his assistants, my memories of him remained vague. He was only one of many coaches who came to see me perform in my senior year at Spruce High School.

When he joined the university, the decision garnered a fair share of intrigue and controversy. He had left the University of Michigan amid the Final Four tournament, causing many people to question his motives and dedication. Albeit, he transformed the basketball program and gained widespread recognition. By the way, the University of Michigan won the national championship in his absence. That championship victory further enhanced the mystique surrounding his career. As a player under him during his remarkable comeback, it was rewarding to witness his ascent to fame firsthand. Coach Frieder's extraordinary skill and dedication led the school to become a top college basketball team in a short amount of time.

The signing ceremony was not as extravagant as I always dreamed of. Instead, it was a simple yet meaningful event in Ms. Betty Brown's counseling office. I looked my best, having donned a fresh haircut, bright orange Pumas, a matching warm-up suit, and a thick herringbone gold necklace.

Also in attendance were my mother and Coach Rhodes. Though the ceremony lacked the glamor of flashing lights and cheering fans, it was enough for Stevin. However, Hedake yearned for something more remarkable.

Interestingly, Hedake accompanied me during my first day of practice. Allow me to clarify. Stevin Smith is the respectful, humble, church-going individual who shaped who I am today. Hedake is the flamboyant, self-assured basketball player and ladies' man who sought wealth, fame, and complete control over the game. Hedake is the one who led me into trouble.

After graduation, it was time for me to move on. In the sweltering heat of the summer of 1990, I bid farewell to my mother, who bravely held back tears as I embarked on my journey from Texas to Arizona. The realization that I was about to leave her behind was frightening, but I knew it was time for me to mature and embark on this new chapter. When I arrived, a representative received me at the airport and took me to the renowned Senora Center. It stood as the newly built, state-of-the-art building that housed the freshman dorm assigned to me. Looking back on it now, I had a lot more than what I lacked. I always stayed clean with the freshest gear, drove nice cars, and kept money in my pocket. In fact, I had six different cars, starting with the Jeep I purchased after my freshman year. I never had a want for anything, and I never missed a meal.

That differed from how I grew up. However, for years, people have wrongfully assumed that my upbringing made me desperate and hungry for material things. Some people said I was quick to sell my soul to the devil for money; but that wasn't the case. From the time I learned how to make my money, that's exactly what I did. And that was whether it came from shooting dice on the streets or accepting gifts from boosters and other "interested parties."

When people ask me how I managed to not only survive but thrive in life, I've always responded with a particular phrase. It came from my late cousin, Mookie. "Cuz, things understood need not be explained," he often said to me. In my case, it meant that I should not always be obligated to explain my life, my decisions, and why I made the choices I've made in life.

Students often form first impressions of college and lifelong friendships, the first day of college. Sometimes it happens during the freshman orientation. Assistant Coach George McQuarn took on a father-figure role. Contrasted to what I experienced with Scooner, he was a great man, a brilliant coach, and a fantastic father to his children. That included his daughter, Tracey, who was once married to R&B singer Babyface, one of my favorite artists. He blessed me by inviting me to dinner along with Tracey, and his wife, Jeretta. That is another one of the legacy stories that are part of my collection. I fondly speak of them from time to time.

The late Coach Lynn Archibald was another influential assistant coach. I didn't talk to Coach Archibald as much as I did with Coach Frieder and McQuarn, but he still made a good impression on me. To this day, I continue to maintain a connection with his sons, who also embody the same admirable qualities as their father.

Although Coach McQuarn could be quite a demanding figure, he played a crucial role in my growth and development. Throughout our time together, he consistently challenged me, and never hesitated to push me to my limits. Indeed, people knew him for his use of strong language; however, having experienced similar treatment at Spruce, I was no stranger to that kind of environment.

Much like Coach Rhodes, Coach McQuarn aimed to break me down. Little did he know, I already possessed the fortitude necessary to face any challenge ahead of me. My resolve to prove my worth to Coach McQuarn and the team was unwavering. I possessed a determination strengthened by the guidance of Coach Richardson and Coach Rhodes. They taught me to remain resolute in the face of verbal aggression. I adopted an air of unshakable composure, and I often responded with a simple, "Yes, sir!"

That effectively showed him and everyone else, my focus and commitment to the task at hand. This approach served me well throughout my freshman year at ASU, where I found success both on and off the basketball court.

Life at ASU brought its own set of challenges, as I was now separated from my family and forced to navigate an unfamiliar environment. My teammates had more family visits than me, which made me feel more independent. Faced with the responsibility of making important decisions on my own, I bolted into the role of a mature, self-sufficient individual.

Undoubtedly, my journey now marked a significant transformation in my life. I was a young man hailing from South Dallas and Pleasant Grove and raised by a single mother. The experience of going to one of the largest universities in the world was both challenging and insightful. The student population was nearly 75,000. Just for reference, the population of South Dallas/Fair Park was estimated at 31,918 in 2023.

Upon first arriving at ASU, it did not take long for me to establish myself as a prominent figure on campus. As the saying goes, "the cream rises to the top." That statement seemed fitting for my situation, as my prominence appeared unstoppable. However, I would soon discover that this notion was misguided and that my rise was not as certain as I had initially believed.

In the early days at ASU, I met Jamal Faulkner, a fellow freshman who hailed from New York. Jamal stood out because of his height. He was easily noticeable at six-foot-seven, and he had a slender build. He had a thick New York accent and bore a striking resemblance to the character J.J. Evans from the classic television series *Good Times*. That only added to his unique presence. Through Jamal, my path soon crossed with that of Benny Silman, a key figure who would ultimately have a significant impact on my life.

From our initial encounter, what stood out most about Benny was his appearance. He was a thin, large-nosed, white youth who possessed an accent surprisingly similar to Jamal's. He also shared Jamal's knack for smooth-talking. Given that we both had a Theater Arts class together, it was only natural for Benny and me to become acquaintances both on and off campus.

Between my academic and athletic commitments, I scarcely had any time left for a social life. However, I would occasionally carve out some time on Sundays—my designated "off day"—to explore the surrounding area. This often led me to venture to either the south side of Phoenix or South Mountain Park, both in a less reputable part of town. They were approximately 15 minutes away from campus. We followed the coaching staff's advice to stay away from Las Vegas, regardless of it being only a four-hour drive from our university. We remained clear of any potential distractions that might have arisen from visiting such a location.

Benny and I met sometimes at social events on campus, where mostly white men were present. He had gained a reputation as the campus bookie, a detail that held little significance to me given my primary focus on excelling in basketball. Before the emergence of the scandal, my financial interactions with Benny were minimal. They were made up of several transactions involving $20 on Sega Genesis games.

I spent most of my freshman and sophomore years at basketball practice, and I had little free time. My determination to succeed was intense to the point that seeing my family, including my mother, became a rarity during my first year of college. For the most part, I could only see them during brief holiday breaks and a summer home visit. I maintained regular communication with Mama, MaDear, my cousins, and Carl Jr., who studied at the University of Miami on the opposite coast.

My spare time was quite limited, and I primarily engaged in recreational activities only if they pertained to romantic pursuits. That subsequently led me to face further challenges. Christy Calvin, my first girlfriend at my new school, was attractive and had a toned body from playing sports. In the past, we colloquially referred to such women as "yellow hammers."

Christy genuinely possessed a kind nature, an affable personality, and an admirable spirit. She was the daughter of Mack Calvin, the assistant coach for the NBA's Los Angeles

Clippers. Her basketball knowledge captivated and intrigued me. During my first year, she was a big supporter, and she came to most of my games and made scrapbooks of my best moments. Our mutual hobby led me to meet her father, but my excessive confidence caused issues in our connection. A diverse range of women seemed drawn to me, and that provided me with many opportunities for romantic encounters. My girlfriend's father knew Coach McQuarn, who offered me cautionary advice at the beginning of our relationship. He reminded me of her father's well-established status in the NBA and urged me not to jeopardize my own aspirations. However, I ultimately failed to heed his warning, and our relationship ended during my sophomore year.

My complete devotion to my basketball career, left no room for commitment to any one person. My priorities placed fidelity on the back burner, while my passion for the sport consumed the forefront. I stayed focused and disciplined for a while with the help of a remarkable positive influence, Janis Frieder, the wife of my coach, Bill Frieder. Coach Frieder's wife, Janis, played a crucial role in helping me earn a place on the dean's list during my freshman year. She was a kind-hearted person, and we shared a unique bond that transcended racial and socioeconomic differences. She was much like a surrogate mother to me, and she offered nurturing support, motivation, and genuine care. I appreciated the fact that she saw the real me—Stevin, the respectful and charismatic individual. She did not see the Hedake persona, who often appeared on game day and during my unsupervised moments.

One of my greatest regrets, once the ASU scandal became public, was not telling Mrs. Frieder how grateful I was for everything she did for me. That devastated me. I could not apologize to her personally after the news broke. She faced significant repercussions that came from my actions and from being Coach Frieder's wife.

When I look back, I consider my freshman year to be the most formative period of my life. Although I perceived myself as a grown man, I discovered my true maturity only after I learned to stand on my own. I no longer had the comforting support and protection that Mama, my family in Dallas, and Coach Rhodes, once provided.

Besides relationship issues, a few teammates and I faced a challenge during our freshman year when we got implicated in a calling card incident. Coach McQuarn, a man of integrity and compassion, kindly provided me with his phone card to ensure that I could regularly contact my mother. He explicitly instructed me to only use the card for that purpose. However, because of my stubborn tendencies, I shared the card with a teammate, who subsequently passed it to another. Over time, the card became shared among several individuals.

It did not take long for the phone card to transform into a communal resource. Eventually, Coach McQuarn summoned me, and I discovered we had accumulated a staggering $16,000 phone bill. The anxiety and guilt overwhelmed me, as I feared my actions might cause my coach to lose his job. Nevertheless, I took responsibility for my actions. I believe other individuals in the same situation would have done similarly. I confessed to taking the card, which led to suspension for myself and a couple of my involved teammates.

This suspension required us to miss a few games and complete community service hours to repay the debt. My greatest distress resulted from my disappointment in myself for betraying a man I grew to love, respect, and admire. I was fortunate that Coach McQuarn forgave me. I learned about being accountable and taking responsibility for my actions.

The situation served as an opportunity to learn how to face challenging circumstances with integrity and maturity.

Once the initial disappointment of the calling card incident subsided, Coach McQuarn and I worked to restore our trust. We wanted to foster our father/son-like bond. My freshman year concluded on a high note; however, during my sophomore year, many heart-to-heart conversations ensued. One particular discussion remains etched in my memory.

After practice one day, he asked to talk to me privately. He asked, "Son, why do you want to play this game?"

As we tossed the ball back and forth, I grappled with his motive and the expected answer to his question. Puzzled, I responded, "What do you mean, Coach?"

He reiterated his query, "Why are you here, and why do you play this game?"

Astonished, I said, "Because I love it, Coach."

I thought he of all people, already knew. His subsequent response affected not only the trajectory of my game but also my life. He earnestly retorted, "I respect you, and I respect your answer, son. However, how can you love something that can't love you back, Hedake?"

Once more, he left me bewildered. He dribbled the ball a few more times before passing it back to me.

"Tell the basketball that you love it," he said, as he folded his arms and stared me down. Dumbfounded, I hesitated. I doubted the effectiveness of this suggestion.

Eventually, I succumbed to his request, and with the basketball in my hand, I muttered, "I love you." I glanced up from the basketball, and I could sense Coach McQuarn's intense gaze. Understandably, I felt embarrassed. The coach then pointed out that the basketball could not match my feelings. I caught his stare as I looked up and felt stupid.

"You don't hear anything do you, boy?"

"No, sir."

"Now tell me you love me."

It was easy for me to look him in the eye when I said, "I love you, Coach," because I meant it.

"I love you too, man. I mean it. But you gotta play the game, not because you love it, but play the game for someone you love, who can tell you they love you back."

I had no reservations about confessing love for my coach because it was genuine. I felt love for him in my heart. Coach McQuarn returned my feelings, but then he imparted the most important lesson in sports. "Play for someone you love who could acknowledge your love and hard work." This exchange inspired me to dedicate my basketball career to the first and only woman I loved at that point—Eunice Mae Smith (EMS). Every time I picked up a basketball after that, I was determined to honor her. A tattoo on my left arm, serves as a constant reminder of my dedication: "Doing it for EMS."

Larry Johnson, Stacy Augman, Stevin, and George Ackles at Stevin's UNLV visit.

Stevin was a standout player at H. Grady Spruce High School.

Stevin is featured on The Boys First Team and was voted Player of the Year.

CHAPTER 5: I THANK YOU FOR IT ALL

Giving back involves a great amount of giving up.
—Colin Powell

I returned to Dallas for the summers after my freshman and sophomore years in college to be with my mom and to feel at home. My basketball game had reached its peak, and I could now focus on my mother and our shared dream of making it to the NBA. We were both determined to see this goal eventually come to fruition.

Following my junior year, I was honored to be selected for the 1993 USA FIBA Under 22 World Championship Team. The opportunity afforded me limited free time, even so, I volunteered my time between the cities of Charlotte and Sacramento. In these locations, I had the privilege of working with children at the renowned basketball camps led by Larry Johnson and Spud Webb. This would also allow me to return home and take part in the Redbird Collegiate League, established by the late Coach Alex Mudd Gilliam.

Coach Gilliam had a renowned ability to attract college scouts searching for potential talent. I appreciated the opportunity to travel and encounter different environments, even though I had a busy schedule. This consistent busyness also ensured that my impulsive alter-ego, Hedake, stayed out of trouble. My mother and I couldn't arrange regular visits during those summer months because she was working at the telephone company. She would come home only for brief periods to rest and recuperate. Typically, by the time she returned, I would either be busy with my activities or resting on my bed, trying to catch up on the sleep I rarely got at the university.

Growing up, we were members of Griggs Chapel Baptist Church, in the Fair Park area of "Sunny South Dallas." This historical house of worship was founded in 1892 under the spiritual leadership of Rev. A.R. Griggs and Rev. A.R. Watson. The members named the church after Rev. Griggs, and they chose Rev. S.E.J. Watson as the church's first pastor.

From a young age, I attended church, and around the age of 10 or 11, I wholeheartedly accepted Jesus Christ as my personal Lord and Savior. This spiritual connection played a significant role in shaping my life's journey.

My mother was extremely devoted to attending the church, and she seldom missed a Sunday service. For her, the church represented a sanctuary of peace and comfort during any season of life. Even during those rare occasions when she could not attend, I continued to go.

One of the many valuable life lessons I learned from my mother, besides her obvious work ethic, was the importance of having a steadfast faith in God. Relying on His guidance through periods of joy and triumph, as well as times of difficulty and adversity, became the cornerstone of my life. This belief was as essential to me as developing my skills in sports and proved to be an enduring life principle. I even encouraged my friends to attend church with me, hoping they, too, would benefit from this foundation.

Griggs Chapel, under the spiritual leadership of Rev. H.D. Webb Sr., provided me with my initial exposure to the world of prayer and worship. My time there fostered a deep affection for gospel music, which remains my favorite genre to this day. The church also served as a platform for me to discover the beauty of expressing emotions through song, a practice that has continued to enrich my life.

Of equal importance, Griggs Chapel instilled in me discipline and self-control, both on and off the court. There was no room for disrespectful behavior within its walls. Initially, my mother would ensure that I sat right beside her during services. As I grew older, she granted me the privilege of sitting at the back of the church with my peers. Yet, even then, I was conscious of my mother's watchful gaze, which kept a proverbial eye in the back of her head.

The widely known saying, "It takes a village to raise a child," emphasizes the significance of a supportive community in a child's upbringing. To raise a well-rounded individual, it takes support from many people. That includes family, church members, neighbors, coaches, teachers, and friends. When I reflect on my life, I see that the people who had the most impact on me came about via divine guidance.

One of these heaven-sent individuals whose impact on my life is far more precious than any accolade I have ever achieved, is my dear friend, JB—short for James Brown (not to be confused with the singer). JB is like a friend, brother, and spiritual advisor to me. The spiritual aspect of his role developed later.

Our first encounter took place during my younger years in Pleasant Grove. JB lived near the apartments where my family was evicted. As the local paperboy, he would occasionally offer my mother, whom he fondly referred to as "Mama," the "homegirl hookup." This included free newspapers and other items he could get his hands on. JB's family was one of the poorest and roughest in the neighborhood, nevertheless, his demeanor and, more importantly, his capacity to love, belied his difficult circumstances. Apart from the four-year gap between us, we formed a strong bond that transcended our obvious differences. Our connection grew to the extent that he became not only a mentor and brotherly figure for me but also a beloved son to my mother. The affection between the two of them was deep and genuine. People like JB show how important community connections are in shaping someone's life. Acknowledging and valuing those who help us grow and prosper is crucial as relationships become more significant.

"Sometimes, one must confront their fears," he advised me one day. We had started running in the neighborhood, and then, without warning, he broke out into the main street, and we ran against the cars, against oncoming traffic. This was his unique method of assessing my courage and character. I trembled with fear, but I completed the task and proved myself to him.

Regarding work ethic, JB was unparalleled, save perhaps for my mother. He would often jest that I could accomplish any task I set my "large head" to. One of his favored adages resonated with me. He often said, "Rise from sedentary complacency and embrace the challenges, foregoing idleness to pursue success. If you labor while others rest, they shall beg as you feast."

In addition, he taught me how to drive. He was also the person I excitedly confided in when I experienced my first intimate encounter, mere months prior to beginning high school. He had many brushes with the law, but still, JB avoided incarceration. The fact that he found himself in trouble was ironic, given his relentless efforts to keep me on a righteous path and prevent me from falling into a life of crime. Regrettably, even with his guidance, I ultimately found myself behind bars.

JB was always there to support me and was notably the first person to confront my father when he failed to keep his promises. One particular incident upset my mother enough for her to confide in JB, which led him to confront Scooner on our behalf. I had grown accustomed to Scooner's disappointments, but my mother and JB felt the hurt I experienced. The details of the confrontation were unknown, but JB chose not to go through with his complete planned attack on Scooner. To his surprise, my father's sincerity and charisma led them to find common ground, referred to by JB as "an understanding."

Throughout the years, I've realized that I lacked nothing during my upbringing. The support of my friends built my life, including Slowpolk, JB, Carl Jr., Trae, T. Turner, A.T., Big Rod, Reggie Thompson, Lamont, T.C., Mike Man, Sammy, and Little Bowman. When the ASU incident happened, it was tough to face those who had invested time, love, and wisdom in me. Disappointing these individuals, especially my cousin, Mookie, became one of my greatest regrets. Mookie, whose real name was William Smith, played a significant role in my childhood.

Our close friendship developed when I was around 10 years old, after my mother and I moved to Pleasant Grove, closer to his residence. As an extraordinary basketball player, Mookie was also responsible for linking me to his best friend and renowned NBA star, Spud Webb. He showed me how the principles of basketball applied in real life as well.

Mookie's frequently stated advice was, "You should apply your basketball mindset to achieve success in life, Hed. Keep in mind that the clock never stops, and you only have a limited number of timeouts."

As I reminisce about the enjoyable memories and essential life lessons I shared with him, I continue striving to become the man he encouraged me to be. Mookie's impact on my life is immeasurable, and I remain filled with gratitude.

Eventually, I adopted his motto, "Things understood need not be explained." This saying resonated deeply with me, and I had it emblazoned on a custom-made T-shirt. Considering the great impression Mookie made on my life, I'd like to emphasize several key points from the story. First, our bond taught me how basketball is like real-life, and I learned valuable lessons from it. Second, Mookie showed me how valuable it is to maintain meaningful relationships. Last, a powerful quote like the one he used for his motto, highlights the importance of understanding the complexities of life without requiring extensive explanation.

On that fateful day when my older cousin and I could have a sincere discussion about the events that transpired at ASU, his words revealed our connections. Although he expressed his disappointment, he confessed my actions did not shock him. Our close bond allowed him to understand my patterns and behaviors, even when left unspoken. He could sense something was not quite right, but acknowledged that mistakes often come with consequences. He then informed me in a serious tone, "Hedake, when you do wrong, there is always a price you must pay. But just know I will not visit you in prison. I cannot bear to do it." He kept true to his word. The stark realization of how my choices affected me and my family was challenging to accept in those moments—and can still be difficult.

I last spoke with Mookie on February 10, 2021, when I called to inquire about his well-being. When he answered the phone, I noticed a change in his voice that revealed the struggle he experienced. All the same, we shared a transformative conversation that day.

"I'm in overtime; in a dogfight, cuz," he said.

I replied, "I know man, but know that God loves you, Mookie, and so do I. Keep fighting Smith Boy."

"Smith Boy" was the nickname we affectionately used to address each other. He emphasized the importance of self-forgiveness and detaching from the past to progress. He recited Philippians 3:13-14: "Brethren, I count not myself to have apprehended: but this one thing I do, forgetting those things which are behind, and reaching forth unto those things which are before, I press toward the mark for the prize of the high calling of God in Christ Jesus."

The verse held different meanings for the two of us. For him, it was a reminder of the fleeting nature of life. I found comfort and a sense of direction in those words. Philippians 3:13-14 is a passage in the New Testament of the Bible, written by the Apostle Paul. In these verses, Paul talks about forgetting what lies behind and straining forward to what lies ahead. He shares his approach to life and faith—not dwelling on past achievements or failures, but focusing on the future. He expresses his goal to press on toward the goal for the prize of the upward call of God in Christ Jesus. This means he strives to live according to God's will, with the aim of reaching heaven.

That is my goal. As a constant reminder, I got an abbreviated version of the quote tattooed on my arm: "Forgetting what is behind and straining towards what is ahead." This has been my guiding principle over the years.

People often say, "If I knew then, what I know now." Talking to Mookie as life drained out of him was one of the hardest challenges in my entire life. Little did I know I would have a similar conversation two and a half years later with someone else who meant the world to me. But God was preparing me even then. As was customary in our conversations, we concluded by expressing our love and appreciation for each other. "I love you, Smith Boy," I said.

He responded confidently, "I love you more, Hedake, and never forget that I am the oldest and the coldest." Indeed, he was. We honor the memory of William "Mookie" Smith, also known as Smith Boy. Unfortunately, Mookie's metaphorical clock stopped ticking on March 10, 2021, when he succumbed to cancer at age 60. His passing left an indelible mark on me, and even mentioning his name brings a painful lump to my throat.

May he rest in power.

1993 USA FIBA Under 22 World Championship Team.

Lamont, JB, and Stevin.

Mookie and Spud Webb.

Mookie and Spud Webb.

CHAPTER 6: WE FALL DOWN

Character cannot be developed in ease and quiet. Only through experience of trail and suffering can the soul be strengthened, ambitioned inspired, and success achieved.
—Helen Keller

My return to Arizona State University for my junior year in the fall of 1993 was a significant turning point. Everything was coming together and my NBA dreams were taking shape. Lester Neal and I secured our off-campus accommodations. Our friendship had formed during my sophomore year, and we were practically inseparable. As most basketball players did, we arrived on campus a week before the start of school and our official season. Lester and I shared many similarities, finding a connection in our common backgrounds; he hailed from the south side of Chicago, while I was from South Dallas. We both grew up in single-parent households and Coach McQuarn recruited us. Our gameplay was alike in style and intensity, even if Lester was a post player and myself a point/shooting guard.

We spent most of our spare time together, often in the company of our teammate, Mario Bennett. Our strong bond, combined with the way we played and the friendly banter we shared, led to our little trio earning the nickname "24-42-44."

This time period highlights the significance of friendship and shared objectives in sports. It also emphasizes the often overlooked worth of similar experiences and backgrounds. The connection between us serves as a testament to the power of friendship in overcoming obstacles and working towards a common dream. For example, we all aspired to have careers in the NBA. It also highlights how friendships, formed in pursuit of a shared passion, can have a lasting and profound impact on one's progression.

When at home, we often occupied ourselves by playing games on the classic Sega Genesis console. As the saying goes, time flies when you're having fun, and our junior year went by without incident, filled with endless amusement.

By the time I began my senior season, I had established myself as a leading basketball star in the Pac-10 Conference. I was indeed a veritable force to be reckoned with on the court. As the year began, NBA discussions frequently mentioned my name and it seemed quite promising that someone would draft me. Until then, I had stayed out of trouble and maintained a moderate lifestyle, focusing on my future. My priority was

Stevin and Lester Neal.

basketball career over romantic relationships. I wanted to share my future financial success with my mother, rather than with potential "baby mamas." However, in November 1993, I made some regrettable decisions that ultimately led to my downfall.

The turning point was when Rick from Chicago brought up his bet on the Arizona Cardinals vs Dallas Cowboys game. He specifically predicted the Cardinals would beat the spread. Being a Dallas native and an ardent Cowboys fan, I confidently challenged him to back up his claim with money. Rick accepted the challenge and promptly placed a bet with Benny the bookie. Benny was an inconspicuous individual, quite different from the loud and flamboyant crowd we were a part of. He had close connections to college athletes.

The fateful bet that started my descent into sports betting involved the Cowboys, who were 13-point favorites. However, their victory was only by five points, and that resulted in my loss of the $100 I had wagered. To console me, Rick assured me it could compensate me to bet on the upcoming Monday Night Football match.

Eager to recover my loss, I placed my bet on the Buffalo Bills during the Monday Night Football game. They were 3 1/2 point underdogs against the Pittsburgh Steelers. Unfortunately, the outcome was far from what I had hoped, as the Steelers secured a 23-0 victory. This defeat left me in even more considerable debt, several hundred dollars behind in the world of sports betting.

As the weeks progressed, my desperation to win enough money to pay off my debt to Benny only grew. I took risks by betting on any and every sport available, regardless of my familiarity with the game. For instance, I wagered on hockey matches, but I had never played the sport, let alone watched it. The results were disastrous, and I spiraled into the worst losing streak of my life.

My monthly scholarship check, intended to cover my rent, offered a brief respite because I needed nearly the entire amount to clear my debt to Benny. Since I had limited options, I thought about asking for an advance from one of my supporters at ASU. They often gave me money to help me keep up my lifestyle. Requesting this advance, however, presented its own risks. Asking out of turn might raise suspicions among the boosters, and potentially jeopardize the aid they provided. Moreover, I was unwilling to reveal the true reason behind my request, as it could taint their perception of me.

Benny reassured me by stating, "Don't worry about it for now." And he generously offered to let me continue betting on credit, hoping I would eventually break even. We even placed bets on Sega Genesis games, an area in which I excelled. Regrettably, my success in gaming was never enough to help me overcome my financial adversity. Within a month, my debt to Benny accumulated to roughly $10,000.

As December approached, I found myself still buried in debt. Benny remained understanding and composed. One evening, we visited The Dash Inn, a popular bar near the campus. After consuming a few beers, Benny casually brought up a proposal that might resolve my debt and provide extra financial gains.

He explained a seemingly straightforward plan: my task was to ensure that the Sun Devils did not win a game he selected by too large a margin. He emphasized he wanted me to guarantee our team did not cover the point spread, rather than intentionally lose the game. I had never done either. However, fulfilling this condition would cause the cancellation of my $10,000 debt and earn me an additional $10,000. Considering the potential benefits, the decision appeared to be an obvious one for me. The prospect of eliminating the debt that loomed over me was undoubtedly alluring. Yet, it was the additional offer of $10,000 that made it impossible to resist. I had cultivated a habit of sending money to my mother every month. The funds usually came from minor gambling wins or surplus cash from my donations. When someone inquired about the source, I would fabricate stories about having a part-time job or devise other falsehoods. I simply wanted to shield her from unnecessary concern or worry.

Benny, the orchestrator behind the scheme, consistently presented everything as straightforward. He skillfully dodged the term "point-shaving" and never hinted at any wrongdoing that could harm my chances of making it to the NBA. How could I decline? Especially given the opportunity to emerge victorious with a financial gain equivalent to nearly what my mother earned in an entire year. This line of reasoning was my driving force.

Upon confirming my affirmative involvement with Benny, he advised that we needed to wait for a game that offered the perfect conditions. After a two-month search, Benny settled on the January 27, 1994, match against Oregon State. In this game, we were 15-point favorites playing at our home court, and that provided us with an ample margin for error. The most favorable scenario would require me to guard a high-scoring player and intentionally allow him to score points. David Drakeford, one of Oregon State's most formidable shooting guards, was the featured player in this game. The plan was simple: win the game while maintaining control of a specific point margin. On game day, Benny would inform me of that desired range, and leave me with the responsibility of managing the outcome.

Interestingly, I had initially prepared for the shooting guard position during the preseason. However, in the first game of the 1993-1994 season, our point guard, Marcell Capers, suffered a foot injury that sidelined him for the year. This actually worked out in my favor, as I had to step up and take on the point guard role. In this position, I could exert better control over the game, since the ball was mostly in my hands. People widely regarded Marcell as one of the top guards in college basketball. As the point guard, he would typically pass the ball to me, which enabled me to score frequently. Following Marcell's injury, Coach Frieder reassigned me to the point guard position. Isaac Burton took over my former role as the shooting guard.

Considering the circumstances, one cannot help but wonder how different the outcome might have been if Marcell didn't sustain an injury. If I couldn't control the game as a point guard, following Benny's plan would be difficult. The idea of approaching Marcell with the scheme was not a comfortable thought. We enjoyed a great rapport, still all in all, I was uncertain if I could trust him with such information.

In the end, Marcell's injury proved serendipitous. With no need to consider revealing the plan to him and with the game under my control, I impeccably executed Benny's strategy. It was the perfect setup for our team's objectives.

In the days that led up to the Oregon State game, a sense of unease settled upon me. For the first time, I faced the task of shaving points, and I felt ill-prepared because of the lack of guidance from Benny. I resolved to maintain competitiveness by allowing the opposing team to score.

My alter ego, Hedake, sought to console me, and reassured me I wasn't sabotaging our team, but resolving a personal predicament. Benny revealed his doubts about my ability to execute the plan independently. He strongly recommended that I involve another player. To guarantee the success of the operation, it required the help of a shooting guard.

Thus, I approached my friend, Isaac "Ice" Burton, a trusted friend. Isaac's gameplay was as formidable as his nickname implied. I also felt confident in depending upon him, as we both shared an affinity for finer things and possessed a drive for making significant moves on the court. Since he lived in a dormitory on campus, Ice was easily reachable. One evening, I made my way to his residence and requested him to join me in my vehicle.

As one of the few students possessing a car phone, I could efficiently facilitate calls. I quickly explained the proposal to Ice, following Benny's original explanation. First, I addressed him casually, yet earnestly, "Hey young buck, I got a way for you to make some extra cash, but I'm going to need a favor from you."

Isaac simply asked, "What do you need from me?" I knew this conversation would be challenging, as I was about to ask him to compromise his morals for my sake.

"I need you to fix a game by missing a few shots," Hesitantly, I told him and tried to minimize the gravity of my request. Isaac, a man of integrity like Stevin, was highly resistant to the idea of participating in any dishonest or immoral activities. Aware of the situation, Hedake stepped in to reason with Isaac. He shed light on point-shaving and the monetary gain it could bring.

Desperate to convince him, I explained, "We won't be losing, man. All we have to do is win the game, but by less." My aim was to simplify the concept and emphasize my belief that we wouldn't be doing anything profoundly wrong. At the same time, I kept my immense debt troubles to myself. That ensured Isaac remained unaware of the high stakes involved.

I acted in good faith and as a means of encouragement, provided Isaac with $2,500—part of the cash advance Benny gave me. Once he accepted the envelope filled with hundred dollar bills, his expression confirmed his commitment to the plan. That's when our infamous partnership started, and we became much like Batman and Robin. In the moments leading up to the game, I received an unexpected phone call from a man Benny had introduced as his associate. People also thought he was a mob connection, a man who would guarantee the success of the deal. He requested a conversation to clarify how the plan would unfold. While I did not know him, I consented to discuss the matter with him. Little did I know at the time that this man, Joe Gagliano, and I would form a powerful relationship.

My aim remained unchanged, even with the tempting offer of $20,000 per game. It was crucial for me not to disappoint my family. I was determined to complete my commitment and then dedicate myself fully to preparing for the NBA.

On game day morning, Benny contacted me to relay the vital information: our team had to ensure a victory while winning by no more than six points. In addition to being projected to win by 15 points, Benny and Joe required a buffer in the event the odds shifted before their wager.

During the pregame warm-up, I battled anxiety in order to maintain focus. Unfortunately, I found no opportunity to inform Isaac of the plan between Benny's call and our practice session. However, during practice, I conveyed the message to Isaac discreetly by whispering, "The number is six." His subtle nod confirmed his comprehension and intention to execute accordingly.

My performance that night was unstoppable, even though I had an injured right pinkie. I scored an impressive 28 points in the first half, successfully making seven out of eight attempted three-pointers. Though my game was great, inadvertently, I increased our lead beyond our predetermined goal. When I came to that realization, I had to remind myself to moderate the game's pace.

At a lead of 40-27 and with the game on the verge of a complete rout, the coach ultimately removed me from play. In a matter of mere minutes, the Beavers had impressively reduced our lead by half.

Exceptional shooters can estimate the amount of space required for an excellent shot by other shooters. Subtly, I adjusted my defense by stepping back half a step from my typical position when guarding a skilled shooter like Drakeford. That provided him with sufficient room to make his shots without arousing any suspicion. As I strategically enabled Drakeford to land open shots, the point gap gradually closed.

Our team emerged victorious with a score of 88-82, winning by six points—a margin that was essential for us to secure the enticing financial reward. Personally, I achieved a career milestone by scoring 39 points, successfully making 10 out of 16 attempted three-pointers. There were no apparent indications of my actions influencing the game's outcome or final score.

Following the game, Benny and I convened at my residence, where he presented me with a Nike shoebox brimming with hundred-dollar bills. The rest, as the saying goes, is history.

Stevin at Arizona State University.

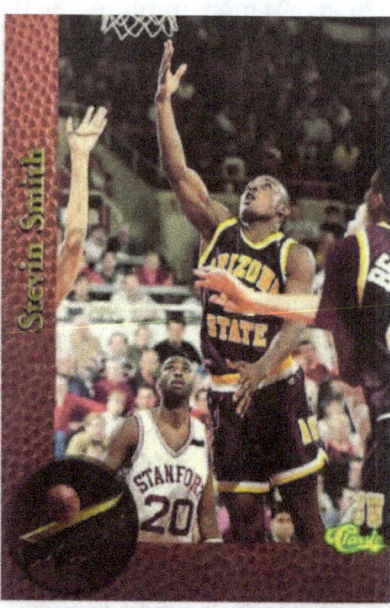

Snapshots of Stevin Hedake Smith player cards.

CHAPTER 7: FEAR IS NOT MY FUTURE

You are who you are when no one is watching.
—**Stephen Fry**

In the wake of my initial point-shaving episode, I experienced an immense sense of relief. Not only was my debt to Benny settled, but I also had some additional funds at my disposal. Per the agreement, I immediately handed over $5000 to Ice as his share. Benny then selected our subsequent home game against Oregon, set for January 29, 1994, as the next target. We were favored by 11 1/2 points, and I assured Ice a reward of the same amount if we achieved the desired outcome.

For this game, Benny instructed us to win by six points or fewer, a directive we successfully followed, resulting in a final score of 84-78. My objectives remained consistent, though my methods of achieving them differed this time. I didn't do well on defense on purpose, but my offense suffered because I twisted my ankle by accident. The injury caused significant pain, which led my coach to remove me from the game. After my ankle was taped in the locker room, I resumed my position on the court. I relied heavily upon my instincts and honed survival skills. Simultaneously, I kept my focus on the financial motivation and rectifying the outcome of the previous game. My performance yielded only 13 points. Ice, too, did not deliver a powerful showing. Yet, combined, we accomplished our shared aim.

After the game, Benny handed me a substantial sum of $20,000 in cash. I immediately provided Ice with his fair share. Without hesitation, I spent about $7,000 on items such as jewelry, clothing, and other objects of my desire. I also sent a generous amount of money to my mother, along with a promise to deliver my GMC 1500 short bed truck to her as soon as possible. In the meantime, I made a significant down payment on a sleek, jet-black GMC Typhoon.

However, my reckless behavior did not cease there. Hedake's actions instilled a false sense of confidence in me, which led me to use a portion of my newfound wealth to place additional bets. One such bet included our February 17, 1994, home game against UCLA, in which we did not take part in any point-shaving. Being the underdogs at 3 1/2 points, I audaciously wagered $20,000 for Benny to bet on our team.

As the game neared its end, we trailed by six points. In the last moments, I seized a loose ball and hastily attempted a three-pointer. Successfully making the shot would have guaranteed me an additional 10 stacks; however, failure to do so meant I would owe Benny the same amount. Although I gave my utmost effort, I faltered and missed the shot, thereby finding myself indebted to Benny for another 20 bands. As much as the Stevin in me wanted to retire from point-shaving, I ended up committing myself to another two games, to keep my head above financial waters.

In Game 3, our team faced the University of Southern California (USC). We had previously defeated them by a significant 25-point margin in Los Angeles. For this match, we were the favorites to win by nine points at home. Confident in my abilities, I informed Benny that I felt capable of handling this game single-handedly, without Ice's help. My underlying motive, however, was that I needed all the winnings for myself, as I found myself in an insurmountable financial rut. Because of that, Ice was not involved in this match.

Unexpectedly, the Trojans showed exceptional performance in the game. They maintained their momentum without any influence from me. It was unnecessary for our team to lose for me to collect my winnings, but we ultimately lost, with a final score of 68-56. Although the defeat disappointed me, receiving a sizeable sum of hundred dollar bills eased my frustration. My mindset shifted to one that mirrored Hedake's. With only a few games remaining in the season, I wondered, *why stop now?*

The last game I agreed to fix for Benny was on March 5, 1994, against Washington. This match held great importance for me because Benny pledged to use the $20,000, he would pay me to bet on this game. If our team emerged victorious by 11 or fewer points, I would receive a substantial payout of $50,000. I found it peculiar that the target point difference Joe and Benny had initially given me continually changed. It went from eight to six, five, and eventually three. Joe's parting words ominously cautioned me to ensure the final game score was a three-point difference. That foreshadowed the imminent complications that awaited.

My focus was on the game and what I had decided would be my final payday. Unaware of the behind-the-scenes drama that had transpired, all I knew was that our team's performance was disappointing. Out of 14 attempts, I missed four shots. We trailed by 11 points. Our poor performance had little to do with point-shaving and more to do with ASU's notorious tendency for terrible stretches. Though difficult to admit, I must confess that my considerable financial stakes in the game meant I didn't give my all on defense.

By halftime, our team had regained the lead, albeit by a small margin of two points, 25-23. Coach Frieder seized every opportunity during time-outs and particularly at halftime, to reprimand us. We performed so poorly that the crowd booed and TV announcers made fun of us. They even suggested we were trying to lose on purpose.

In the locker room, Coach Frieder wasted no time voicing his frustration. "You guys are playing terribly!" he shouted. "We have NBA scouts present tonight, so if you don't pull yourselves together, you can wave your NBA careers goodbye. Furthermore, I received a call from the FBI stating that this game is under investigation."

I did not look up, but his words captured my full attention. He persisted, "You better inform me now if you all are aware of or involved in whatever is happening out there!"

At that moment, I understood that in order to deflect any suspicion about my involvement, I had to step up my game. My goal was to win the game by any means required, and to tackle the subsequent consequences, whether financial or otherwise, at a later stage. Unbeknown to me, the line had shifted a staggering 44 times. The Nevada Gaming Commission was called upon by the authorities when they noticed the significant change. Matters escalated, and soon enough, the FBI was involved as well.

The overwhelming realization that I might have jeopardized my NBA career made me physically ill. I could not help but think about Benny and Joe and the sheer volume of bets—potentially amounting to millions of dollars—they must have lost. With my NBA aspirations at stake, I had to prioritize my own interests and those of my family. I ensured we emerged as victors in the game.

Afterward, I discovered that every bet Benny and Joe had placed that night resulted in a loss. Indeed, Joe had suffered losses in the millions. I also learned that Benny had informed several of his gambling acquaintances about the fix. This caused them to place frantic bets against ASU in various venues throughout Las Vegas. And that resulted in even greater financial losses.

However, I must admit that my hands were not entirely clean in this situation either. I had informed another friend and fellow ASU student, who will remain anonymous, about the fix. This friend was a kindhearted person who treated me well and had a passion for betting. He had the resources to place bets, although his luck proved rather unfortunate. The primary reason I shared this information with him was my desire to help him out and my knowledge that this would be my last fix. What I did not expect, however, was that he would inform several other friends, neglecting the vow of secrecy I had asked of him.

The officials and Las Vegas sports bookies did not overlook the irregularities. Both entities suspected foul play. One of the odds-makers contacted the Pac-10 to share his point-shaving suspicions because of the fluctuating spreads. Soon, it all came crashing down.

I now see that no amount of money from Benny or Joe was worth endangering my NBA career. On that fateful night, I hastily and discreetly left the arena after the game. When I got home, I saw Benny standing outside my building like a bodyguard. He was upset. As I drove up, he walked up to my vehicle, and motioned for me to lower the window. When I did, he shouted, "What the hell happened, Hedake?"

He wasn't alone. He was accompanied by his imposing enforcer, Big Red—a fitting nickname for a man weighing nearly 400 pounds. They informed me that Benny had vouched for me, and that led Big Red to gamble a significant sum of money on the game. It terrified me, particularly when he demanded the repayment of his losses. He wanted a hefty $75,000, or else I would face severe consequences.

Desperate and without options, I assured Big Red that upon signing with one of the NBA teams and receiving my bonus, I'd settle the debt. Fortunately for me, satisfied with my promise, he departed with Benny, and granted me a temporary reprieve.

However, relief was short-lived. A little while later, a phone call from a team trainer summoned us all back to the activity center for an emergency meeting. With a feeling of dread, I hurriedly dressed and returned to campus, determined to maintain my composure. Coach shared the startling news: the FBI suspected point-shaving in our game. He claimed knowledge of the perpetrator's identity and urged confession. Convinced it was mere intimidation, I remained stoic and unaffected. As the meeting ended, I departed without having any suspicions directed towards me.

As Isaac followed me, we found a safe space where he nervously inquired, "What do we do, Hed?" I could sense his anxiety, but I maintained my composure for both of us.

"Don't say anything to anyone," I advised him. "I believe this situation will diffuse itself on its own. We just need to stay composed."

Unfortunately, my assumption quickly proved incorrect. The following day, an onslaught of stories emerged in local newspapers. Each one suggested that someone had rigged the Washington game. A day or two later, Benny contacted me, explaining he intended to leave town because of the increasing scrutiny in Phoenix. He reiterated my obligation to pay my debt, but insisted I remain silent. That conversation marked the last time we spoke.

By the subsequent Monday, the news had escalated. National newspapers and television stations bombarded the public with news about the "unusual bets" on the game. Coach Frieder showed immense support for his team by claiming none of his players were involved in wrongdoing. As for me, I did my utmost to avoid drawing attention to myself in the aftermath of these events. As I contemplated my future, I reassessed the choices I made. Eventually, I decided it would be in my best interest to follow Benny's example and distance myself from the situation. As difficult as it was, I withdrew from all of my classes and packed up as much as I could fit into my Typhoon. Then, I embarked on a 15-hour journey, back home to Dallas. In doing so, I left behind my dignity.

The thought of not graduating, although still being close, continues to cause me distress. However, I find solace because I departed as an accomplished athlete. I held the title of leading scorer in basketball history at ASU and earned the designation of Male Athlete of the Year. This esteemed recognition placed me ahead of other noteworthy ASU attendees like renowned golfer, Phil Mickelson and NFL star, Jake Plummer.

An eerie silence—no inquiries, no phone calls, and not even the perception that I had vanished from ASU—marked my initial months in Dallas. This unsettling realization left me feeling apprehensive.

To avoid dwelling on the events that transpired, I focused on keeping my mind occupied. There was not much need for concern, as nobody mentioned the situation. Apart from a few phone conversations with Lester, I received no calls from Coach McQuarn or Coach Frieder, nor from any of my teammates, including Isaac. Our last communication had centered on both of us lying low and remaining silent.

As the date of the NBA draft approached, my focus shifted from the recent troubles to this pivotal moment in my life. It was a turning point. I had worked tirelessly on it for more than a decade. This was an occasion that deserved a celebration, and alongside my mother, we took it upon ourselves to plan an enormous party. The idea was for it to be one that would not only commemorate my dreams but also bring our community together.

On June 29, 1994, our three-bedroom house on Ella Street in Pleasant Grove saw an influx of well-wishers. Our entire neighborhood gathered around our big screen TV in eager anticipation of the NBA Draft. My mother had proudly ensured that she took care of every detail. That included hanging handwritten poster-board signs created in her beautiful penmanship. Some signs congratulated me and acknowledged her pride, and others invited and welcomed family, friends, and neighbors.

My mother left no stone unturned. She fried a sufficient amount of chicken and cooked enough fixings, it seemed, to feed half of Pleasant Grove. Many guests answered her request to contribute side dishes to this remarkable occasion. Her excitement was contagious, and her voice often echoed through the streets as she proclaimed the news to passers-by, "My child is about to be drafted!"

With the opportunity to be selected by one of the 27 teams taking part in the draft, I remained optimistic as they announced the first few picks. My name hadn't been called yet. Our community's support and lively atmosphere helped us remain composed. We stayed hopeful while indulging in the scrumptious food and enjoying each other's presence. As the center of attention, I mingled with my guests, and didn't sit until the latter half of the first round. At this moment my nervousness escalated. Frowning images of Big Red, undoubtedly watching from across the country, invaded my thoughts.

At the conclusion of the first round, my name remained uncalled, and a nauseating sensation emerged in the depths of my stomach. With every team that bypassed selecting me, I became increasingly convinced that the NBA officials had discovered my hidden past. This growing certainty weighed heavily on my mind.

As the second round progressed, the once vibrant atmosphere significantly diminished, and the guests gradually departed. Eventually, I found myself almost alone in the room. Upon hearing Zeljko Rebraca from Serbia declared as the 54th and final pick, only Mama and a few others remained. I avoided eye contact with her. Her expression of disillusionment and despair was too heart-wrenching for me to face. Feeling suffocated, I craved fresh air and solitude. I fled the scene after I climbed into the driver seat of my GMC Typhoon with no inkling of my destination or ensuing actions. All I recognized was the urgent need to escape in order to clear my thoughts. Humiliation and a sense of hopelessness overwhelmed me. The feelings left me shattered and penniless. They utterly crushed my aspirations of providing Mama with a better life away from the hardships of the 'hood, and a fresh start in a new home.

How do I explain this to Mama? I pondered as I navigated the winding roads of Dallas for what felt like an eternity. During my time at ASU, I maintained a low profile. Be that as it may, I always appeared affluent and fashionable. Most people remained unaware of my true circumstances—they simply didn't suspect that I didn't come from money.

I desperately needed to reevaluate my choices. Looking back on my life and the decisions that led me here, I recognize the value of having intelligent and insightful individuals in my life. Astute and financially literate people in your life can be a great asset. Their knowledge and insights can guide you in making wise financial decisions. They can also help you understand complex economic concepts and inspire you to improve your own financial literacy. Most of them have valuable advice on saving, investing, and managing money based on their experience and expertise. They can introduce you to their networks, opening potential opportunities for growth and collaboration. Being surrounded by such individuals can elevate your financial understanding. They may also stimulate your intellectual curiosity and critical thinking abilities. I now understand that it would have been wiser to avoid the temptation of quickly amassing wealth through deceit or shaky deals.

I could have put the additional money I received from supportive fans to better use. I now realize that investing in the stock market would have been a more responsible choice. If I had followed the footsteps of individuals like Uncle Ural, I could have used the returns to pay off my mother's mortgage and secure her future.

But life teaches us invaluable lessons, and I'm grateful for the wisdom gained over the years. Once, I took pride in my intelligence, but as I transitioned from smart to wise, I valued wisdom as well. I now resonate with the words of my Uncle Ural Lee Smith. He said, "A smart man sees what they are showing him and hears what they are saying, whereas a wise man sees what they are not showing him and hears what they are not saying. A smart man learns from his own mistakes, whereas a wise man learns from the mistakes of others."

CHAPTER 8: STAND

You have power over your mind, not outside events. Realize this and you will find strength.
—Marcus Aurellus

After being subject to an "epic draft fail," I found myself at the center of gossip alleging that I was involved in a gambling ring and took part in point-shaving. These rumors eventually made their way back to my small Dallas community. Whispers grew, though still, I maintained my innocence. I resolutely denied any involvement in such activities. Those who knew me well and understood my deep love for the game believed my side of the story. However, it appeared the NBA remained unconvinced.

The ongoing situation occupied my every thought, and plagued me both day and night. I even experienced nightmares related to the ordeal. What puzzled me the most was the reason behind these sudden suspicions about my character. Throughout my time at ASU, I flew under the radar and maintained a low profile during all four games. I displayed none of the telltale signs associated with point-shaving. I didn't make wild passes, take poorly aimed shots, or miss free throws. I strategically avoided such acts because they are the most obvious indicators of a dishonest player. These signs are precisely the ones everyone looks for when scrutinizing potential foul play. No one—not

Coach Frieder, Coach McQuarn, or even the FBI—had ever approached me with any concerns regarding my conduct. With my record as ASU's top scorer, team captain, and Male Athlete of the Year, it was implausible to suspect me of wrongdoing.

However, I couldn't help but wonder if my hasty departure from campus had triggered unwanted attention and led people to connect the dots between my actions and the gambling allegations. The entire experience was bewildering. It served as a monumental wake-up call for me, and it spotlighted the need to move forward since basketball was all I knew. Unwaveringly, I vigorously hit the gym and trained harder than ever.

Directly after the NBA draft, I received a much-needed lifeline. It came as a call from the Cleveland Cavaliers. They extended me an invitation to their training camp. Overwhelmed by the opportunity, I did not think twice before accepting the offer. I hastily departed for Cleveland, eager for a chance to shine on the court. Immersing myself in my passion provided a temporary refuge from the recent ordeal; however, my NBA dream shattered once again when I failed to secure a spot on the roster.

A higher power seemed to have other plans in store for me. In a surprising turn of events, during the final day of camp, a team in Spain presented me an opportunity to play for an astounding $25,000 monthly salary. I seized this incredible offer, and within days, I joined Team Somontano Huesca, a prestigious Spanish basketball team.

After spending two enriching months in Spain, I made my triumphant return to the United States in pursuit of more challenges. I joined the Continental Basketball Association (CBA) during the 1994-1995 season, and represented the Grand Rapid Hoops in Michigan. Upon the completion of my debut season, I traveled back overseas to compete in the Philippine Basketball Association (PBA). There I proudly played for the Sunkist Orange Juicers. My exceptional performance earned me the distinguished "Best Import" award. That honor recognizes the top American player in the league.

However, life had another unexpected challenge waiting for me. While thriving in my basketball career, I received the devastating news that doctors had diagnosed my mother with colon cancer. Heartbroken, I stood by her side as she underwent surgical procedures to remove as much of the cancer as possible. An arduous journey through chemotherapy followed.

I was earning approximately $40,000 a month, a testament to how far I had come within the sport. During that period, I sent money home to my mother in order to help her with medical expenses and bills, since she could not work for about a year. Once that season ended, I returned to the CBA to play for Grand Rapids for the 1995-1996 season. A major change occurred that season, though; we had a new head coach, Brendon Surr, who had been an assistant coach with the Detroit Pistons.

Coach Surr's arrival marked the beginning of a challenging time for me on the team. He aimed to recruit new talent, and this meant I had to prove myself all over again. One day, I received a call from the team owner, who summoned me to his office. He praised my style of play and expressed the team's desire to keep me on board. However, tough choices were necessary.

The owner explained they could only reserve a spot for me on the team by placing me on the suspended list, but they would continue to pay me. I took little time to make what I believed to be a wise decision. Even though I needed the money, I also knew my worth and did not want to compromise it by accepting a place on the suspended list when I could absolutely play. It quickly became apparent to me that the CBA lifestyle was highly competitive. They could replace players without warning or any reason. However, it helped me financially, and enabled me to support my mother during her tough battle against a serious illness. I felt grateful for the opportunity to earn a living by doing something I loved.

Although the Grand Rapids team released me, I was soon picked up by the Sioux Falls Skyforce. When I arrived in South Dakota, I instantly became a fan favorite and felt fortunate to be a part of one of the top CBA teams. Our games consistently drew sellout crowds, and the fans' enthusiasm reminded me of my time at ASU. After winning the CBA Championship in 1996, they asked me to return for another season, which would be my last in the league. That year, they drafted Dallas native and basketball standout, Jason Sasser, to join our team. They later chose me for the All-Star team, which was a significant achievement.

In March 1997, I experienced my worst game in the CBA with seven turnovers and I went 0 for 14 from the field. However, as the saying goes, bad days don't last forever. Following the game, I received a call from my agent, Jeff Blakely, who had previously represented Spud Webb and had been my first agent after leaving ASU. Expecting the worst, I braced myself for the news that I was being cut from the team—but the call took a surprising turn. Blakely informed me I would soon head home. However, he surprised me by sharing the news that the Dallas Mavericks had offered me a ten-day contract, and that overjoyed me. As fate would have it, Erick Strickland, the point guard for the Dallas Mavericks, suffered a broken hand and could not play for the rest of the season.

"Thank you, Jesus!" I exclaimed, boarded the first available flight from South Dakota, and joined the Mavericks in Atlanta for their game against the Hawks. I felt an incredible sense of triumph and accomplishment, having climbed my way back to the top. To commemorate the occasion, the team treated me to a first-class flight and limousine service. When the team's trainer handed me my per diem, I couldn't help but reflect on the journey that brought me to this point. Particularly, I thought about the costly decision that significantly set me back.

At that moment, however, I felt as though I had finally escaped the lingering shadow that had hung over me for the past three years. The feeling only amplified the belief that I had successfully put the point-shaving scandal behind me. I had made it to the NBA. *They can't touch me now*, I naively told myself. Little did I know the storm brewing in the background would soon arrive with full force. It would bring along the challenges I never could have expected.

During my time with the Mavericks, I was fortunate enough to sign the maximum allowed two 10-day contracts. The twenty days spent playing for my hometown team were an incredible gift that I am eternally grateful for.

One of my most cherished memories from my brief tenure in professional basketball was the moment I received my team jersey. The exquisite fabric felt as delicate as I envisioned a cloud would feel against my skin, and its fragrance was akin to my imagination of heaven. Though I only could play a handful of games wearing the prestigious #1 jersey, I will eternally be thankful to God for granting me a taste of my ultimate dream. As a member of the Mavericks, I achieved the prestigious honor of an ESPN Play of the Day with an awe-inspiring half-court shot against Golden State. I also had the unique chance to share the court with the legendary Michael Jordan, which was beyond my wildest dreams.

However, as the adage goes, all good things inevitably come to an end. With less than a week left in the 1997 season, my second contract drew to a close. Upon its expiration and the conclusion of the season, it delighted me that the Mavericks were interested in inviting me to training camp. Words cannot convey the emotions I experienced at that moment. It felt as if a wave of relief washed over my body and invigorated my soul.

I thought about celebrating with my mom, buying her a new house, and paying off my debts. Yet, as another age-old saying cautions, "What is done in the dark will always come to light."

I can attest to this harrowing experience as a mere day or two later, I received a phone call no one wishes to receive. It marked the tragic end to what I believed was a fresh start in my life.

"Hello?" I hesitantly answered my mobile phone, which was quite unusual for me when it came to blocked, unknown, or unidentified numbers.

"Do you know who this is?" the mysterious voice on the other end inquired.

"I know who this is," I said because I recognized the voice immediately.

"Do not mention my name on this line."

Although I knew the voice belonged to a certain friend, I will not name him in my story. Initially, I assumed this to be a tasteless joke, but as it transpired, the matter was serious.

"An old college acquaintance will call you tomorrow," my friend proceeded gravely. "He will contact you from the Dallas airport and will extend an invitation for a meeting. Should you accept, be cautious and touch his left leg. He is wearing a wire. He is collaborating with the FBI."

I only had time to utter, "For real?" before my friend cut off the conversation. This was a scene directly from a movie.

Remarkably, the following day, I received the ominous call from a fellow alumnus of my college. It was an individual who had placed a bet on ASU after he heard about my ill-advised tip regarding the point-shaving scheme for the Washington match.

He said he was at the airport and wanted me to come by to talk about "that stuff in college." I knew it was a set-up, but I headed for the airport, anyway. When I got close by, I pulled over and dialed his number.

"You can kiss my !@#$%, and you can tell your friends who are listening in from the FBI that they can kiss my !@#$% too, because I ain't coming!" I said.

Later, I found out my so-called friend had made a deal with the FBI in exchange for telling on me. Feeling pressured, I panicked, and immediately called my agent and told him what was going on. He advised me to get a good lawyer. I did, but not soon enough because not even a month after that episode came the knock at the door I'll never forget.

It was the summer of 1997 and a typical scorcher of a day in Texas. Mama and I were at home relaxing when the doorbell rang followed by hard knocking. I answered it to two white men, dressed in suits. Had it not been for the anonymous message I got on my pager earlier in the day, which simply stated, "THE FEDS ARE COMING," I would have been completely blindsided. Just like I knew who they were, they knew my identity. They obviously saw Mama stirring in the background and asked if we could go somewhere and talk privately.

"Who is that?" Mama inquired loudly as she approached me from behind.

I found it impossible to look directly at her or respond to her question. Bypassing me, she headed straight for the door to investigate the situation herself. I believe the three most dreaded letters anyone could ever encounter, besides "IRS," are "FBI."

"Well, do you have a subpoena?" she questioned.

"No, but we can get one if necessary," replied one of the mysterious men in black suits, without any hint of hesitation or a suggestion of amusement. The response evidently conveyed the gravity of the situation to Mama, as she immediately ceased her opposition, and the two agents and I walked outside.

Soon, we found ourselves in the nearby Pemberton Hill Recreation Center Park. We sat on park benches near the gym and the agents presented a posterboard displaying eighteen images. Among them, I recognized only my face, and the faces belonging to Benny and Big Red.

"This operation extends far beyond you, Stevin," one agent remarked. A white man using my legal name made me sweat even more in the scorching sun. "You cannot comprehend the number of people involved, and within this group, you hold a relatively insignificant position," he continued.

The second agent spoke solemnly and said, "Someone has manipulated you heavily and you don't understand how deeply involved you are in this matter."

At that moment I realized the seriousness of the issue at hand. I ran out of excuses and time; the truth finally caught up with me. For the next 45 minutes, I tried my best to maintain composure while listening attentively to everything they said.

At the end of the discussion, I asked them, "Are you finished with me?"

"Yes, but we'll see each other again," one of them responded.

"You'll likely need a lawyer," the other cautioned as our conversation ended.

It became clear that they had thoroughly investigated my case. One of them even had the audacity to ask whether I would prefer to inform the Dallas Mavericks about my "minor predicament" myself or have them do it on my behalf?

When I returned home, I found my mother anxiously waiting on the porch, with tears streaming down her face. For all the attempts to comfort her with reassuring hugs, forehead kisses, and promises that everything would be fine, my words fell on deaf ears. I knew deep down that our current situation demanded an open and honest conversation—one that I had been avoiding for almost three years.

Incomprehensible as it was, nearly three years after I orchestrated my last fixed game at ASU, my basketball career seemed to near its end. Just as my dreams of joining the NBA were materializing, I stared down at the possibility of a prison sentence.

Indeed, someone said, "Good news travels fast, but bad news travels even faster," and that holds true. It wasn't long after the FBI paid me a visit that I received a call from the Dallas Mavericks' general manager, Donnie Nelson. He inquired about my involvement in the scandal. As soon as I confirmed it, he severed all ties with me until someone cleared my name. He wanted to avoid negative media attention. My dream of playing for my hometown team and achieving my basketball aspirations slipped through my fingers once again.

However, there was one more person I held in high regard whom I had to inform about the turn of events—Coach Rhodes. He played a pivotal role during my senior year, acting akin to a personal agent. Coach Rhodes took and made calls on my behalf and provided me with valuable advice. If not for him, I may have never progressed as far as I did in my career.

When the scandal at Arizona State University broke and the situation escalated, I decided to have an honest conversation with Coach Rhodes. I needed to talk to him like I did with Coach Richardson. As a man of integrity, it was important for me to disclose my actions.

After completing another season of playing basketball overseas, I returned to Dallas to prepare for my trial. I knew well that Coach Rhodes had continued to follow my career and occasionally sent me messages through my mother. He, like many others, had expected my selection in the first round of the NBA Draft.

The scene remains etched in my memory even today; a vivid recollection from a distant past. The walk towards the gym felt like the longest journey of my life that day. I felt like I was walking towards my doom on the "green mile," just like a condemned prisoner.

As I neared the gym, the thunderous sound of basketballs pounding against the wooden floor echoed through the halls. The distinctive screech of Jordans accompanied the noise on the surface. The anticipation of meeting Coach Rhodes was overwhelming, as I wondered about his reaction. Would I receive a barrage of profanities like in the years gone by, or would he embrace me with a hug, a firm handshake, and a few words of encouragement? Or would he simply send me off to confront the consequences of my past actions?

With a bittersweet feeling in my heart, I walked into the gym adorned with many awards, plaques, and photos bearing my name on the wall. As I entered the gym's double doors, I saw Coach Rhodes with his back turned, deeply engaged in a practice session.

He enthusiastically called out plays and offered advice to the young players, who bore a resemblance to me, albeit with seemingly less skill at their age. His completely engrossed demeanor prompted a few players to notice me and stare with a hint of recognition. Coach Rhodes remained focused on the ongoing practice, only turning around upon hearing the call of his name.

"Coach Rhodes!" I shouted with my hands cupped around my mouth to amplify the sound.

He spun around and graced me with his familiar, comforting smile. "Hey, here!" he exuberantly declared. Then, he addressed his team. "Gentlemen, please take a break." As they dispersed, I couldn't help but notice their knowing glances, showing they were aware of my identity.

He embraced me warmly, seemingly ignorant of the brewing gossip and the approaching tempest. Our embrace was solid and heartfelt, like two individuals truly elated at reuniting. Afterward, we proceeded to a vacant section of the bleachers. Having exchanged cordial greetings, I felt it was time to tackle the subject that loomed between us.

"Coach, I need to tell you something," I said with difficulty, struggling to maintain eye contact. "I want you to know that you taught me right." The subsequent admission was emotionally taxing for both of us. We sat in silence, and it felt like minutes rather than seconds. Coach broke the quiet, heavy with my tears, with his reassuring and empathetic response. I will never forget his words because they were a beacon in my darkest moment.

"Hedake, man, you're gonna get through this. I promise. We're gonna get through this… because I have faith in God that He will see you through this."

Later that night, the news of the point-shaving scandal exploded on ESPN, signaling the collapse of my world as I knew it.

Stevin's short stint with the Dallas Mavericks was a dream come true.

CHAPTER 9: SILVER AND GOLD

Tis better to have loved and lost than never to have loved at all.
—Alfred Lloyd Tennyson

It wasn't long before I found myself abroad once more. During this period, I encountered my first struggle with depression. If it had not been for the faith ingrained in me from a young age, the overwhelming pressure might have caused me to crumble. However, I persevered. I concentrated on the grace God had granted me in the form of freedom—even though I knew that my time as a free man would soon draw to a close.

This is a glimpse into the workings of the professional basketball world. When looking for new players, most overseas teams behave like predators and scout for exceptional players who were recently let go from the NBA. As it turns out, I was at the top of this list of sought-after players. Within a few days, I received calls from my agent, agents representing other players, and various interested parties. They enticed me again with the prospect of playing basketball overseas.

At first, a mix of embarrassment, pride, and ego prevented me from taking action. Truthfully, the turn of events shamed Hedake, while Stevin understood the necessity of making a move. This was because the bills demanded payment, and more importantly, God willed it. After the FBI showed up at my door, I heeded their advice, as well as my agent's, and got legal representation. I secured the services of George Klink, a prominent Arizona attorney who other agents and individuals highly recommended. My attorney talked to the US Attorney's office in Phoenix after my meeting with the federal authorities and made a deal. To seal it, I had to give a written statement about my involvement which granted me some much-needed extra time. However, this extension did not come with any guarantees of avoiding prosecution. That made my time and decision-making even more crucial.

After three months of introspection and contemplation, I made a pivotal decision to join Team Olympique in Antibes, France. They offered me a lucrative contract worth $125,000, which assisted with my soaring attorney fees that ranged from $7,000 to $8,000 per month.

Turmoil raged back home, but my experience in France was nothing short of incredible. The French culture, particularly the food and breathtaking views, left a lasting impression on me. What stood out the most, however, were the people and their unique way of greeting each other with a kiss on each cheek. Inspired by the beauty and intricacy of the French language, I embarked on learning it and, before long, became fluent. As a black athlete living on the French Riviera, I enjoyed a life full of respect, love, and certain privileges.

During the summer of 1997 in Antibes, I encountered basketball legend Micheal Ray Richardson. Unbeknown to me, he would become a consistent and guiding presence in my life. Living and playing in Antibes and meeting Richardson had a big impact on my journey.

You should know him if you have a basic understanding of basketball and followed the legendary players of the 1980s. Nicknamed "Sugar" or "Sugar Ray" at the pinnacle of his career, he was an electrifying presence on the court for the

New York Knicks and New Jersey Nets. He emerged as one of the most dynamic point guards of his era. However, his story is also one of downfall, as he, like me, struggled with issues. His battle was with drugs. Unfortunately for both of us, our troubles unfolded in the public eye. Michael Ray's exceptional basketball skills were something I admired and that led to our eventual friendship.

Similar to me, everyone knew Michael Ray for his bravado on the court. He, too, had a humble upbringing in a single-parent household. His family was an enormous responsibility, with five siblings and a mother who relied on him after his father left.

Michael Ray had a dream, not unlike my own—to achieve great wealth, purchase a new home for his mother, and enable her to leave her job. Following his draft to the New York Knicks in 1978, he honored his dream and bought his mother a house.

Regrettably, Michael Ray succumbed to a crack cocaine addiction, a tragic turning point in his life. He once had a million-dollar contract within reach, but the grip of addiction hindered his progress. He underwent many stints at rehab centers and attempted comebacks, yet still, his career came to an abrupt end in 1986. The final straw was when he failed a drug test that led to a permanent disqualification from the NBA.

When we first encountered each other, he was in his forties, playing professional basketball in Bologna, Italy. He competed with and against players young enough to be his children and he maintained a powerful presence on the court. Throughout our interactions, he consistently displayed graciousness, humility, and a willingness to offer support. An all-star in the NBA who experienced the heights of success, he lost it all but kept the mentality of a champion. His resilient spirit inspired me to believe that I could also overcome my challenging circumstances.

In my first year playing basketball in France, I achieved an average of 17 points, 7 assists, and 4 rebounds per game. The lucrative contract I signed was quite rewarding, considering the time. Our team got ready for the season with a strict schedule. We had two-a-day practices for six weeks to improve our physical fitness. The season ended with our team winning five games in a row, but we still didn't make the playoffs.

During this tumultuous period, I was grateful to spend Thanksgiving and Christmas with my mother and the rest of my family in Dallas. I faced the looming prospect of imprisonment because of my legal entanglements but most people had no idea.

At that time, I encountered the mother of my middle daughter. We met at a popular nightclub in Dallas owned by Deion Sanders, Prime Time 21. As we continued to talk, I arranged for her to visit me in France, and this is when we conceived my lovely daughter, Kayla Trenae Smith. At this point, a child was certainly not something I expected or wanted. However, I had always been candid about my intentions with any woman in my life.

In this situation, both of us had been reckless. Deep down, I believe that God's timing is impeccable, and His plan is devoid of errors. This conviction makes me thankful for my daughter, Kayla, and the decision to welcome her into this world.

In the summer of 1998, upon my return home, I felt an overwhelming sense of my world collapsing. My attorney lost faith in the possibility of reaching a deal with the authorities, and I appeared to be in financial disarray. My expenses included legal fees, supporting my mother, and providing for Kayla's mother, who was about to give birth within a few months.

My first encounter with an angel from heaven above, named DD, a.k.a. Delicia Lavette Green, led to a momentous change in my life. Her father managed an office, where one of her co-workers, Po Bill, organized a tournament I took part in during summer breaks. He requested I visit the office to collect a team jersey.

As I walked past, I glimpsed a captivating woman. Although I had traveled extensively to various countries and witnessed the beauty of many exotic women, DD had an aura about her. It caused that distinct "butterfly effect."

With an exquisite face featuring a large, yet most charming mole, she stylishly sported a short haircut reminiscent of the actress Halle Berry. To top it off, her perfectly sculpted physique rivaled that of Janet Jackson, and made her the embodiment of perfection in my eyes.

When Po Bill introduced us, I felt overwhelmed with fascination, and it made me uncharacteristically tongue-tied. My smitten state left me with little to say. It caused me to smile and stare. Before leaving the office, I got a business card, and I subsequently dialed the provided number as soon as I left the premises.

"Is this DD?" I inquired apprehensively.

"Yes, who is this?" She responded with the confident, audacious tone that has endeared her to me all these years.

"This is Reggie, the guy who just left."

"I thought your name was Stevin?"

"It is," I chuckled. "I was just testing your attentiveness."

We shared a laugh together.

"Do you have plans for lunch?" I asked, filled with trepidation at the prospect of her declining.

I requested her to meet me at Cheddar's on Interstate 20 and Hampton. And our journey began.

As our comfort levels grew, we felt encouraged to share intimate details about our lives. I divulged information about the complicacies of my baby mama situation, with a child on the way. She revealed she had a daughter, Aerian, who was around two-and-a-half years old. The concept of finding a life partner without children seemed to make a mockery of my plans. However, it showed that our intentions are often at odds with what life truly presents.

    I felt both insecure and comfortable around DD, a feeling I hadn't experienced since middle school. Amid my tribulations, seeing DD instilled in me a renewed purpose. It gave me a glimmer of hope for the future, and made me momentarily forget the challenges I faced. In the beginning of our relationship, I found myself enamored with DD's presence. She revitalized Stevin. Her lack of interest in basketball and my past accomplishments made our connection even more extraordinary. DD claimed to have played basketball, yet her knowledge of the sport seemed limited. Regardless, she fell in love with Stevin, not Hedake, which was refreshing to me.

    Once, I arrived at her apartment, assuming my status would allow us to enjoy an intimate evening. However, her decision to have me sleep on the couch turned out to be a welcome surprise. This gesture of self-respect was in stark contrast to the fans who surrounded me until that point, and it further solidified my attraction to her.

    Not sharing a bed distinguished her from other women who had crossed my path. Rather than seeing it as an inconvenience, this gesture captivated me—it indicated that she was a woman with strong morals and values. And that was exactly the partner I sought. With her, love and communication came easily, conversations were engaging, and she possessed an unmatched sense of understanding. I appreciated our life experiences as we gradually shared our personal stories. This distinction also set her apart and deepened our connection.

As the summer neared its end, I prepared to travel to Turkey. Prior to my departure, a major incident occurred, one that threatened the foundation of our relationship. While driving my Corvette, DD was involved in an accident. Instead of making the repairs, the finance company repossessed the car. DD found herself compelled to raise questions. I divulged to her the details of point-shaving, as well as my own struggles with suicidal thoughts. Her fervent prayers for me, unlike any I had ever received, led her to advise me to place my trust in God's hands, for only He could resolve my situation. Her response ultimately solidified my decision. Her compassionate heart matched her beauty.

As it came time for me to depart from DD and continue on to Turkey, it filled me with both a heavy heart and the determination to return and marry this remarkable woman. In order to show my dedication and sincerity, I purchased her a promise ring. Now, I know this wasn't an engagement ring. Truthfully, I couldn't afford the ring she deserved. But to be clear, a promise ring signifies a commitment to each other. It's often seen as a pre-engagement ring and symbolizes a pledge to a future together.

I could not risk losing her and my desire to build an honest life together. Uncertainty shrouded my future. The looming possibility of imprisonment plagued my thoughts. Mounting legal fees, which accumulated to an overwhelming degree, compromised my ability to provide for DD, her child, Kayla, and my mother.

While in Turkey, we briefly lost touch following the tragic death of her god-brother, Sharone Creer, in a motorcycle accident. It was perhaps the loneliest time of my life. We were geographically separated, still, I endeavored to offer support and comfort to her throughout her period of grief. Our daily conversations provided peace, but the reality of my physical absence during her time of need brought its own pain. With my return home for the holidays, I could finally lend a more substantial hand in her healing process.

CHAPTER 10: FROM HEDAKE TO INMATE# 01044-748

I'd put prison second to college as the best place for a man to go if he needs to do some thinking. If he's motivated, in prison he can change his life.

—Malcolm X

In the spring of 1999, I made a brief trip back to Dallas. Upon my return, an unexpected and alarming situation met me. My attorney instructed me to relinquish my passport, as federal authorities had proceeded with their legal case against me. This marked a turning point in my life, with the most significant event occurring on November 15, 1999.

On the advice of my attorney, I embarked on a fifteen-hour drive to Phoenix to avoid the inevitable media attention I would have faced at the airport. Accompanied by my mother, DD, and my godmother, Carolyn, we made the journey in my mother's Ford Expedition the Sunday prior to the trial.

The night before the trial, sleep eluded me because of the overwhelming fear, uncertainty, and regret that occupied my thoughts. As I dressed the next morning, the realization that it could be one of the last occasions that I would wear a suit for some time weighed heavily on me. I chose a gold-colored suit, complete with a black shirt and shoes. I guess the more conspicuous side of me craved to make a lasting impression in front of the cameras.

OG Ron, Micheal Ray and Stevin.

Stevin and wife, Delicia, aka DD.

I was cognizant that the trial would attract a considerable media presence and curious onlookers. They were eager to be witness to either a great fall or a triumphant resurgence. Clinging to the remnants of my pride, I endeavored to maintain a dignified demeanor as I entered the courtroom. The spectators filled the room with a mix of familiar faces and those of strangers.

The president of the NCAA stood up and requested the judge hand down the maximum sentence to me, which was five years. My legal representative, George Klink, then requested permission to approach the bench and attempted to reason with the presiding judge. He passionately stated, "Judge, I'm not asking you to not punish my client. I'm just asking for you to give him a second chance and not end his career with a five-year sentence."

My lawyer suggested probation instead of jail time because I cooperated with the investigation. Regrettably, Judge Robert C. Broomfield remained resolute in his stance. He argued my actions had caused irreparable harm to the reputation of the university. When given the opportunity to address the court, I earnestly sought to maintain my composure. I expressed profound apologies to my mother, the university, and Coach Frieder.

"I realize what I did was wrong," I said, struggling to restrain my emotions.

That day, I left the courtroom with a one-year and one-day prison sentence for my involvement in sports bribery. Besides incarceration, the judge sentenced me to three years of probation, mandated me to complete 200 hours of community service, and fined me $8,000. Of course, I could not afford to pay the fine. December 13, 1999, marked the beginning of my prison term at a low-security federal facility in Big Spring, Texas.

As we exited the courtroom, a crowd of reporters and photographers surrounded us. They shouted my name and posed questions. Attorney Klink previously advised me to leave immediately following the judge's verdict and to not answer questions.

Once the truck door closed, tears streamed down my face. They were not tears of despair, but rather of relief. A wave of tranquility washed over me, and lifted a tremendous burden I had carried for years. A transformation from listening to gospel tunes to the sounds of Tupac marked the journey back to Dallas. My mother, however, was seething with defiance as she, along with everyone else, knew I was being scapegoated and duped. My sentence outweighed the severity of my crime.

Luckily, I had 30 days to strengthen myself mentally before serving time. Throughout that month, I spent time with Scooter (Eric Tatum). Most of the time we drank and ate Williams Chicken. I found comfort in alcohol and grappled with fear at the prospect of losing my freedom and facing the unknown in prison. As a basketball player who never spent one day locked up, I was ill-equipped for incarceration.

Several of my friends had spent time behind bars, primarily in federal penitentiaries. The authorities had recently released Charles Bailey, a good childhood friend we affectionately called Choo B. During this tumultuous time, he served as a pillar of support. He even drove me to my destination—a remote location amid the plains of West Texas, known as Big Spring.

On the day I had to turn myself in, Choo B picked me up from my mother's house and we headed to South Dallas. There, he purchased a 12-pack of Coors Light. Handing me one, he encouraged me, "Take a big swig, homie."

"Life as you know it is about to change," he warned me, and he couldn't have been more accurate. "Hed, this is now the time to get your life together and come up with a game plan," he said. "Get your life in order, and you will get through this. Don't be too hard on yourself, but maintain your focus. It's more mental than anything."

Indeed, he was right. Choo B and I parted that day after we shared a heartfelt hug and a firm handshake. I turned myself in to serve my time at the Federal Correctional Institution (FCI) in Big Spring, and I went from being Stevin "Hedake" Smith to No. 01044-748. From that moment on, that number identified me, not the name I had tried hard to build and protect.

I hadn't exercised in months, primarily because of the anxiety leading up to my sentence. Consequently, I weighed in at an astounding 294 pounds—the heaviest I had ever been. They gave me a Dickey's uniform, which comprised of a green shirt, green pants, and black combat boots. Then, they escorted me to my unit, which resembled a large dormitory with almost 100 bunk beds. They had stripped away from me every comfort of home.

During the initial three nights, sleep eluded me. I tossed and turned, cried, and prayed—and sought peace in those dark hours. On the fourth day, I finally found an inner peace. How? I accepted responsibility for my actions and ceased to blame others. As I stood there, emotionally, and physically weak, I realized it was time to turn my life around and face the consequences of my actions. I finally stopped pointing fingers and blaming everyone else. Weak from barely eating, I gazed into the clouded reflection of a man with black, saggy bags under his eyes, looking back at me. I was at the lowest point of my life.

I knew I couldn't live that way, and eventually, my mindset finally changed. My faith was my driving force, and it compelled me to fight against the obstacles I faced. And with the grace of

God, I overcame those adversities. I, Stevin "Hedake" Smith (Number 01044-748), had to acknowledge that I alone bore the responsibility for the situation I found myself in. During this realization, something stirred within me and I strove for improvement. I started working out, playing basketball, and doing everything in my power to stay on the right path.

Though it was difficult to accept, being imprisoned was now regarded as one of the greatest turning points in my life. It changed me a lot. I went from being a flashy basketball player named Hedake to a more mature person named Stevin Smith, the way God wanted me to be.

I had ample opportunity for reflection and connection. I encountered many men who shared not only their words but also their wisdom with me. Surrounded by this exclusively male environment day in and day out, my thoughts would often drift toward DD; however, I had to develop the discipline to refocus and control my thoughts. Through this experience, I came to understand the realities of a lifestyle I never wished to endure again.

My days were monotonous from Monday through Friday. The routine primarily revolved around the prison's cabin count ceremony. This event occurred thrice daily: midnight, 4 p.m., and 8 p.m. It involved a guard announcing our designated numbers. Prayer became a calming force in my life. It allowed me to develop a deeper appreciation for the blessings I had. It also allowed me to appreciate the life I hoped God would grant me upon my release.

As part of my path towards reform and growth, I got a job in prison. My employment entailed performing lawn work from 7 a.m. to 3 p.m., and though the work itself was not challenging, the mental adjustment was a significant hurdle. My previous life revolved around basketball. Ultimately, I made it work.

Following my daily job, I engaged in physical exercises such as running on tracks, pull-ups, push-ups, and dips. This fitness regimen earned me the nickname "Mr. PPD." After the workout, I showered and prepared myself for dinner. Although this time was marked by trials and hardships, it was also a time of personal growth and self-discovery.

The structured daily routine played a pivotal role in helping me regain focus and return to optimal condition. While the repetitiveness of this schedule might be overwhelming to some, it provided a necessary sense of stability. Admittedly, the menu was far from pleasing on the palate, yet I seldom voiced my discontent.

Our week usually started with baked chicken and vegetables on Mondays. Tuesdays featured a much-anticipated pizza night, while the kitchen staff reserved Wednesdays for hamburgers. By the time Thursday arrived, I was less concerned with the dinner menu, as that was the day we could purchase items from the commissary. Tuna and chips became a favored alternative to the usual dry spaghetti and meatballs. We informally knew Fridays as "Fried Chicken Fridays." Our weekend dinners usually consisted of beef or turkey, accompanied by rice, potatoes, and a medley of vegetables. We anticipated the meals served each week.

I am grateful to both DD and my mother for their support. Not only did they continuously answer my calls, which allowed me to hear their voices, but they made sure I had sufficient funds on the books. Similar to the free world, there was a cost for everything, like additional food, snacks, and postage for my correspondence.

On the weekends, played basketball or softball without worrying about work. These games often became highly competitive, given the athleticism and drive possessed by many of my peers. They may not have played any sport professionally, but they went after it like they were pros.

When I wasn't at work, asleep, or taking part in physical activities, I devoted my time to various leisurely pursuits. Activities like playing dominoes, card games, table tennis, and pool were available. People could also watch TV in the recreation rooms.

Just as I experienced in the schools of Dallas, the prison environment proved to be one of the most segregated places I had ever encountered. Segregation happened because people did it themselves, not because someone made them do it. My interactions ranged across a diverse group of individuals, except for the Border Brothers—a Mexican prison gang. It was hard to deal with that gang because they always got into fights.

The prison contained three separate TV rooms. On any night, specific racial groups occupied these distinct spaces. The Mexicans would congregate in one room, Caucasians in another, and African Americans in the last. Members of each group typically took part in shooting pool, playing dominoes, or watching entertainment channels like BET.

Nightly, we watched a music video program called Midnight Love. As it played, my mind often wandered towards my future fiancée, with dreams of the enduring love and passion we would share upon my release. Save for a handful of people, most of the individuals in the gathering successfully upheld their traditional masculine image. When music by D'Angelo or any other similarly scantily clad male artists came on, a majority vacated the area with haste. Most of us were uninterested in witnessing such displays.

During my time in prison, I met some of the biggest financial brains and key figures in several major financial scandals in history. One encounter was with an older white man who had quietly been embezzling money from Bank One for years. His method was to take a dollar from every account without getting caught, until finally, an audit revealed his scheme, and he ended up in federal prison.

I also met another guy who was convicted of running a large-scale marijuana smuggling operation. He moved nearly eight thousand pounds of marijuana weekly for years without being caught. He used tractors filled with cannabis. Both men claimed to be millionaires and thought they were smarter than the rest of their fellow inmates.

Instead of flaunting their wealth with expensive cars and jewelry, these guys saved some of their earnings. They also claimed to have invested wisely. They did this knowing that if the authorities ever caught them, they'd still have a financial safety net to fall back on after their release. I must admit that, unlike these financial geniuses, I didn't have any such backup plan. To put it bluntly, I didn't have "a pot to piss in or a window to throw it out of."

During my stay in prison, I received a great deal of wisdom about life from various individuals. There were people like Jigga from New York, O.G. Ray, who faced 27 years, Little Buck with a five-year sentence, and Big Beaumont from Beaumont, Texas. who was in for eight years. They convicted these individuals of drug-related offenses. Since I received the shortest sentence among them, they gave me the nickname "short timer." They believed my crime was relatively insignificant when compared to their actions.

As I served my sentence, time seemed to move swiftly, and I didn't experience any significant issues. At least it did until the day I found myself in solitary confinement for missing work. Feeling unwell that day, I failed to notify my supervisor and simply did not show up. My supervisor, whom I believed harbored racist attitudes, knew my name and the circumstances that led me to jail. He went out of his way to make my life exceedingly difficult. He often assigned tasks meant to break my spirit.

Solitary confinement felt like my personal hell—dark, cold, and underground. For two weeks, I endured 23-hour lockdowns with only one hour allotted for recreation and bathing. With nothing more than a toilet and a bunk bed, I spent my time getting acquainted with God. The prison authorities permitted me to make one phone call per week. During one of these calls, I learned they had cut off my visitation rights.

The day I emerged from solitary confinement, I eagerly sought an acquaintance in the prison kitchen, and implored him to help me find a job. With a little under six months remaining in my sentence, I knew acutely that I could not mentally endure another period in isolation. Although my faith was strong, there was a lingering fear that it might not withstand a second round of such punishment. Yet, I held on to something I heard at church, "God never puts more on us than we can bear." In this instance, it proved true. By granting me a new occupation, He spared me from further tribulations, and I was profoundly thankful for this blessing.

My circumstances shifted from confinement to anticipation, with a mere half a year separating me from freedom. I kept up with my fitness and weight goals while also working on my personal growth, and that made time go by quickly. I intended to be in prime physical shape should God present me with another chance to take part in the only sport I ever loved.

During those last months, my connection to God deepened. I dedicated time to prayer, read His Word, and secluded myself to evade further indiscretions. My aim was to formulate a plan that would ultimately lead to redemption and reward. On the morning of my release in October 2000, I received the most valuable advice of my life from O.G. Ray.

He stated, "If you look back, you'll be back." As he spoke, his jaw trembled, and his eyes filled with unshed tears.

CHAPTER 11: THE STORM IS OVER NOW

We must be willing to get rid of the life we've planned, so as to have the life that is waiting for us. The old skin has to be shed before the new one can come.
—Joseph Campbell

Because my sentence was extended by a day, I had to serve a mere nine and a half months in prison. This time was difficult because I like to be social, but I had to be alone in a new place. Nonetheless, I focused on serving my time with dignity and determination.

Upon my release, they transported me by van from the prison to a bus station. There, I found DD, who had waited patiently to accompany me back to Dallas. Before reporting to the assigned halfway house in Wilmer, Texas, we made a brief stop to attend to some long-overdue, intimate matters.

The halfway house was approximately fifteen minutes south of Dallas. It accommodated around seventy-five men and women. They organized it in such a way that males and females lived in separate sections of the facility. As a condition of my probation, they mandated me to secure employment. I was fortunate to find work in a little under a week, at the office managed by DD's father.

I was fortunate to have full support from my family, which now included DD and her family. My faith in God remained steadfast. Throughout my imprisonment, I was unaware that divine intervention had been working in my favor behind the scenes. Micheal Ray Richardson, whom I had met during my first overseas stay in France, had followed my journey since I became incarcerated. Little did I know, he also played a pivotal role in securing an opportunity for me to return to the French league as a point guard for Antibes.

He contacted me through a mutual friend, Skeeter Henry, and Skeeter contacted my mother. Previously, we hadn't exchanged contact information. Antibes offered me a starting salary of $50,000. Though on the lower end of the pay scale, it provided me with financial independence and the ability to reintegrate into society. Above all else, this opportunity granted me a chance to get back into the game of basketball, both literally and metaphorically. Moreover, it allowed me to make another fresh start overseas.

I can attribute Micheal Ray's willingness to vouch for me to two things; first, he saw similarities between his own experiences and mine. Second, he wanted to pay forward the help he had received when he faced challenges. His act of faith in my abilities proved beneficial, as within a month after my release, divine intervention cleared the way for my return overseas. I could earn a living while doing what I was passionate about.

My unwavering determination to not let my loved ones down again motivated me to train, pray, and focus diligently on every aspect of my life. This dedication resulted in an exceptional performance on the basketball court. And that captured the attention of a team in Nancy, France. They extended an offer for me to join their ranks—an offer accompanied by a substantial salary increase. As a member of the Stade Lorrain Université Club Nancy Basket (SLUC) basketball team, we celebrated many victories. That included the esteemed Courage Cup Champions, an accolade equivalent to an NBA championship. My life was steadily improving, and I was blessed with the opportunity to make amends. Armed with renewed determination, I vowed to prevent the return of my previous self-destructive tendencies.

The amount of time I spent playing basketball in Europe proved essential to my emotional recovery and dedication to positive growth. Europe provided an environment free from the shadows of my past and offered the chance to regain both security and respect. To my relief, I found many Europeans were unaware of the notorious ASU scandal that had once overshadowed my life. They welcomed me warmly, which allowed me to reclaim the sense of self-worth I once held.

After achieving victory in the Courage Cup championship, Asvel Villeurbanne, a prominent team in France's basketball landscape, presented me with an enticing offer. One moment stands out forever in my mind. My dear friend, Sugar Ray, (Micheal) who had unexpectedly taken on the mantle of sports agent, valiantly fought to secure the best possible deal for me. His tactics involved dressing the part. He adorned a Louis Farrakhan-esque suit complete with bowtie, glasses, and a Louis Vuitton briefcase for our negotiations. His efforts paid off as Asvel Villeurbanne agreed upon a two-year contract, with a doubled salary and a $20,000 signing bonus. That evening, Sugar Ray and I indulged in a luxurious steak dinner complemented by a bottle of Cristal to celebrate our victory.

In the following weeks, my beloved partner, DD, and I finalized the date for our wedding, July 30, 2002. She was my unwavering support as Delicia Lavette Green became my cherished wife … Delicia Lavette Smith.

We exchanged our vows in the picturesque backyard of her parents' home in DeSoto, a day that remains one of the most cherished and joyous moments in my life. This milestone signified a resurgence of my personal life and my professional accomplishments as well. Through an act of respect and tradition, I had sought permission for marriage from her father months prior. Although Mr. Green granted it, he presented me with his expansive gun collection. It was a subtle reminder to tread carefully and considerately with his beloved daughter's heart. And this responsibility, I was determined to steadfastly uphold.

After enjoying a staycation-style honeymoon, I returned to France to continue my basketball career. This time, it was in Lyon, playing for Team Asvel Villeurbanne. Life became rewarding for me, and our long-distance relationship allowed us to remain strong as she visited frequently. Our financial future was secure, and that ensured that neither DD, our daughters, nor my mother faced any difficulties from that moment on.

After we were married a year, we decided to have a child. My career blossomed and enabled me to make sufficient money to support my family in comfort. I felt incredibly fortunate to experience life in different parts of the world. Besides France, I played a year in Israel, two years in Russia, and shorter stints in Italy and Bulgaria. While in Israel in 2004, our beautiful daughter, Chloê, was born. Although I loved Israel, two decades ago I didn't appreciate its biblical history as I do now. I was within arm's reach of Jerusalem, the Sea of Galilee, and many other religious sites, but then, I wasn't in the Word of God, at least not to the extent I am now.

Regrettably, in 2008, during a game in Bulgaria, I tore my meniscus while executing a game-winning play. The meniscus is a C-shaped piece of cartilage in the knee that cushions and supports the joint. I had to return home because of the injury, and the doctors prescribed a short and easy six-week rehabilitation and recovery process. The time spent at home allowed me to rest, rejuvenate, and reconnect with friends and family. Unexpectedly, a life-altering event occurred during my recovery period. While at my in-laws' house, I became involved in a friendly competition with my nephew, Darion Green. We shot hoops and performed dunks on an eight-foot-tall goal—significantly shorter than what I usually played on. During my recovery, I still had a lingering weakness in my right leg, and that caused my left leg to compensate for the imbalance. As we headed back indoors, my nephew issued one last challenge, which would prove to have unforeseen consequences.

"Come on, Unc, one more dunk!"

All I recall is attempting the final dunk and experiencing the excruciating sensation when my left leg collapsed beneath me. The impact with the ground was so forceful that I bounced upon contact, and laid motionless until the paramedics arrived. It was the most agonizing pain of my life, and I knew at that moment that my basketball career had come to a premature end.

Initially, I had assumed I had several years of competitive play left in me. However, the diagnosis of a torn anterior cruciate ligament (ACL) dashed those dreams completely. Never did I imagine that my career would end in such an unceremonious fashion. I had aspirations of retiring at the pinnacle of my sport, not because of an injury sustained while dunking on a mere eight-foot backyard goal. Admittedly, this was a tough reality to accept, but eventually, I made peace with the fact my days on the court were over. By the grace of God, other aspects of my life were thriving, such as having a loving wife and family.

During the initial years following my injury, I devoted much of my time to reflection and relaxation. I pondered the rich experiences and countless blessings I had enjoyed. My reality differed from the NBA stardom I once envisioned. Yet, my life remained fulfilling and extraordinary. As people inquired,

"What's next, Hedake?" I didn't have a clue, and that was the harsh reality. This uncertainty terrified me, particularly when my financial reserves dwindled once more. With no source of income, my expenses continuously drained my funds. My partner, DD and I, along with our three daughters, had grown accustomed to a specific lifestyle. I could sense the impending return of my depression. Interestingly, I believe fate, or perhaps divine intuition, alerted DD to the forthcoming change.

Months prior to my injury, she had suggested that we re-evaluate our expenses and reduce them accordingly. She had also urged me to prioritize saving. In retrospect, I am certain that there was some higher force at play, as DD's advice seemed to appear out of thin air. It was as though she possessed knowledge unknown to me. This unexpected intervention served as a wake-up call. I became resolute in my commitment to never be careless with my decisions or finances if granted the opportunity to earn that level of income again. It's not uncommon for people to make promises to God during difficult times, hoping that He will help them overcome their struggles. They often forget many such commitments once their situation improves.

One day, DD shared a profound insight that still resonates with me. "Nothing good will happen to you until you give God His time and attention," she said. "How can you expect God to make a change in your life, our lives, when you're not living right?" At various points, God had presented many opportunities before me. Although they seemed within reach, I couldn't quite grasp them and nothing materialized. He showed what He could do for me if I made Him my priority. Upon deeper reflection, I realized she was correct.

Since being released from prison, although it has taken many years, I progressed from merely believing in God to actively following His teachings. Back then, it was only to a certain extent; however now, I follow Him wholeheartedly. Through a series of trials and tribulations, I slowly began putting God first in my life. I have become more committed; attending church services, paying my tithes, and deepening my understanding of the Word of God. As I made these changes in my life, I experienced a remarkable transformation. By dedicating my time, energy, and focus on God, I noticed significant improvements in my relationship with Him and in my overall well-being. This realization urged me to continue prioritizing my faith and seeking further spiritual growth.

I immersed myself in the Bible, and focused on the wisdom found in the book of Proverbs. My commitment to Christ started during my youth, but it wasn't until I fully surrendered my life to Him, that I truly experienced His guidance and direction. I felt a sense of peace and relief after making this decision, similar to when I confessed my role in the point-shaving scandal years ago.

The transformative power of my renewed faith manifested itself in various ways, especially in my professional life. God gave me many job opportunities, beginning with my role as an assistant men's basketball coach at Mountain View College from 2011 to 2018. I continued my journey by training and mentoring young athletes, and I also started a successful transportation business. Alongside my professional growth, I attempted to address unresolved familial conflicts. I sought to reconnect with Scooner, my father, and develop meaningful relationships with my siblings on his side. Past attempts at reconciliation had been sporadic and insincere. My deepened faith provided me with the humility necessary to forgive him, just as God had forgiven me. When my father's wife, affectionately known as Mama Connie, passed away in 2022, our familial bonds strengthened and deepened further. I was filled with excitement for the re-establishment of these connections in my life. Without my faith in God, I would not have experienced the personal and spiritual growth essential to overcoming my past and forging a brighter future.

Over the past fifty years, I have experienced a constant support system in my life, and I cannot express enough gratitude for this. Therefore, I am committed to celebrating and praising the source of this support as long as I have the breath to do so. It took me some time, but delving into the teachings of the Holy Scripture has provided me with profound insights and enlightenment. I understand that there is a divine anointing upon my life. God has meticulously arranged for certain individuals to be part of His grand design for my life's purpose. All that is required from me to do is surrender to His divine plan and to embody the role He has envisioned for me. One of the critical aspects of this role is to share my story. By doing so, I hope others might find inspiration in it, and potentially make more informed choices.

People ask about my relationship with my former classmates and teammates at Arizona State University. More specifically, they want to know about my relationship with the man responsible for orchestrating the controversial scheme, Joe Gagliano. Years after Burton left Arizona State University (ASU), the two of us reconnected in Las Vegas.

While I coached my Amateur Athletic Union (AAU) basketball team, Burton refereed the games. Our reunion was reminiscent of better days as we greeted each other with a firm handshake and an affectionate embrace. We exchanged phone numbers, yet never spoke again until years later. We came together once more to take part in the Netflix documentary, *Bad Sport: Hoop Schemes* about the ASU scandal.

As for Coach Frieder, it took even longer for me to come face-to-face with him. In fact, it wasn't until 2011 that we crossed paths during the NCAA Sweet Sixteen, West Region Tournament in Anaheim, California. I spoke to students from the University of Connecticut, Duke, Arizona, and San Diego State. During this event, I connected with many rising basketball stars. Among those in the room, were Kawhi Leonard from San Diego State, Kemba Walker from UConn, and from Duke, both Kyrie Irving and Nolan Smith—who all are now NBA players.

"Hello, Hedake," I heard a familiar voice from behind me. It was Coach Frieder, someone I hadn't seen in quite some time.

After we talked for a moment, I stated, "I'm speaking to these young men, hoping to inspire them to make better choices than I did in the past," I responded.

It was an honest and vulnerable moment we shared. He congratulated me on my accomplishments, and expressed his happiness, but also displayed a hint of caution. As we parted ways, I asked him to pass on my regards to his wife and daughter, both of whom had displayed great kindness and care towards me during my time at ASU. He agreed, and we shook hands. Unfortunately, I haven't seen him since.

Coach McQuarn passed away in 2017. Regretfully, I didn't leave ASU on the best of terms, and I failed to give him the respect he deserved by saying a proper goodbye at that time. It weighed heavy on my mind throughout the years. However, I was fortunate enough to get a second chance to make amends. In the summer of 2013, I ran into him in Las Vegas. I was in town for an AAU tournament that coincided with my visit. Grateful for the opportunity, I had dinner with Coach and Lester, a friend I had remained in contact with over the years. We still communicate regularly.

"Coach, I must apologize to you," I began, only to be interrupted by his reassured voice.

"Man, Hed, you don't need to apologize. You know I still love you, man, and always will," he told me. "Hey, you made a mistake. You were a hell of a player and as much as I hate how things went down, you have bounced back well and I want you to keep pushing, man."

Coach McQuarn was a noble individual whom I deeply respected. His approach to life and the assistance he provided to those like me were commendable. Years ago, I experienced an unplanned encounter when Coach McQuarn visited his daughter, Tracy, in Dallas. Tracy was dating NFL Hall of Famer, Deion "Primetime" Sanders, the current football coach at the University of Colorado.

This was certainly a full-circle moment that showcased how life works in mysterious ways. Deion was looking for someone to lead the basketball program for his organization, Truth. Without hesitation, Coach McQuarn recommended me for the position. Thanks to his endorsement, I coached AAU teams for the remarkable Deion Sanders.

People believed Joe Gagliano was the mastermind behind the ASU scandal and held him accountable for his actions. He received fifteen months in prison alongside three years of parole, one hundred hours of community service, and a $6,000 fine. God's plan brought us exceptionally close as friends, even though it seemed unimaginable. Joe is undeniably one of the most relaxed and level-headed individuals I have ever met.

Since our reunion in Waco in 2020, we have cultivated a friendship that transcends common understanding. My bond with Joe helped me find forgiveness. It was not only for those involved in the scandal that affected us both. There was forgiveness for Joe, and crucially, for my own actions.

Over the years, our friendship has grown stronger through countless conversations. He often invites me to attend some of his family gatherings, and we have shared many meals. Joe introduced me to a close friend of his, who is now a dear companion, Reverend "P Mac." I gave him that nickname. My relationship with Reverend P Mac developed into a spiritually entwined connection that has been a true blessing for both of us.

People often inquire about how Joe and I transitioned from adversaries to close friends, considering the tumultuous journey we experienced together. They also express curiosity about whether I feel resentment or anger towards him, as our lives took divergent paths in the scandal's wake. My response is simple: no. I firmly believe God has crafted a unique plan for everyone. I am confident that with unstoppable faith, diligence, and perseverance, my time for redemption is forthcoming. I am determined to keep on pursuing and grinding towards a positive future.

As I reflect on my journey, I express my gratitude to Jesus for His guidance and protection throughout my life. Without His watchful presence, I believe the darker forces might have led me astray. It has been a lengthy and arduous process, but my appreciation remains steadfast. My faith has facilitated my growth as a father, but also as a husband and mentor. In these roles, I strive to inspire and uplift those around me, always learning and seeking new ways to better myself.

CHAPTER 12: PERFECT PEACE

Like a good chess player, Satan is always trying to maneuver you into a position where you can save your castle only by losing your bishop.
—C.S. Lewis

Over the years, I've heard many variations of the saying, "Sometimes you have to lose in order to win." I must admit, as someone with a winner's mentality, it was difficult for me to comprehend this quote. Almost everyone I know groomed me for winning all of my life. My trophies, awards, and newspaper clippings can attest to that. Yet, it's not only me. To a great degree, America, the country I grew up in, focuses much of its attention on winning. The seven principal founding fathers did not risk their lives to go down in history as losers. George Washington, Thomas Jefferson, John Adams, Benjamin Franklin, Alexander Hamilton, John Jay, and James Madison, bet everything they had in order to win. And now, 249 years after the signing of the Declaration of Independence, Americans often put winning above everything else...often even above God.

America has always had a strong emphasis on winning and success. This idea is driven by the belief that these are measures of one's worth. The culture in the US emphasizes winning and achieving excellence in various fields, such as sports, academics, and business. Being competitive can motivate people, but it can also cause stress and pressure. To be fair, winning is an important part of life that is often emphasized in many cultures around the world. Other countries consistently emphasize success and achievement in sports, academics, business, and other activities. Society has instilled this focus on winning into us since childhood, through families, schools, and even media. But to paraphrase an old, popular commercial, no one said, "I want to be a loser when I grow up." Losing for me was a paradox. Not that I was victorious all the time. However, when the final buzzer went off and my team had fewer points on the scoreboard than our opponent, I had a sickening feeling in the pit of my stomach.

What could anyone possibly mean by saying, "Sometimes you have to lose in order to win?" The answer came one day through DD. As corny as it might sound, she has been my one constant, my rock, that has kept me from losing my sanity. Understand, I'm not putting her on the level with God. I know without a doubt, God worked through her to deliver me here on earth, through the most difficult times in my life. And she's still here.

******

DD's Viewpoint

There's a certain term people use, and it's called divine intervention. It is the belief that a higher power intervenes in our lives to achieve a particular outcome. For thousands of years, people have believed in divine intervention, which is when an external force makes sense of a difficult situation. When something seemingly inexplicable happens, we see it as God's way of showing us the path forward or saving us from harm. This divine force helps us overcome hardships and create better lives by guiding and helping us. Some people view divine intervention not as a literal action taken by a higher power, but as an inner voice guiding us toward the right decisions. We can see this in moments when we make life-altering decisions based on an intuition that comes from beyond ourselves–even if we don't understand it. These experiences make us think that something mysterious, like a guardian angel or divine energy, is involved in our lives.

When facing difficulties, people rely on faith, prayer, and meditation to build a relationship with higher powers. Believing in divine intervention is a choice. Prayer and other spiritual practices can bring us peace during difficult times, regardless of our beliefs about divinity. For me, all I can say is "But God."

When I met Hedake, I was at work. At age 20, I was pretty much self-sufficient. I had a place of my own. And I took care of myself and my two-and-a-half-year-old daughter, Aerian. For sure, I wasn't looking to get into any type of serious relationship. I was at that age where I was still trying to figure life out as far as what I wanted to do. Because I didn't know what I wanted to do, I left school, came back home, and started to work. I grew up in a two-parent working household as the youngest and only girl among three boys. I come from a blended family. My parents loved on everyone. Our house was always open to other children.

At the office my dad managed, one guy who worked there, also held basketball tournaments. He always walked around talking about "Hedake this!" and "Hedake that!"

Finally, I asked, "Who is this Hedake guy?" He really loved Hedake and couldn't believe I didn't know him.

"You have never heard of Hedake?" he asked.

It shocked him. He must have felt like I had been hiding under a rock. But that's the truth. I had never heard of him or Stevin Smith, Stevin L. Smith, Stevin Lamarcus Smith, Stevin "Hedake" Smith, or plain ol' Hedake. And it wasn't like I knew nothing about basketball. I played the sport in high school, but like many people, I did it to potentially use it as an avenue to get into school.

"Nope, I don't know him," I confessed.

"Well, I'm getting ready to have a tournament, and he is heading up here to get his jersey. You'll get a chance to meet him when he comes up here." He only wanted to introduce us. He wasn't trying to hook us up, and that was fine with me. Hedake was coming in because he was playing on his team and that excited him to no end.

"Okay, that's fine," I nonchalantly said. When he came into town, Hedake made his way to the office to get his uniform. My co-worker introduced us and the conversation was cordial.

He said, "Nice to meet you."

I said the same, but I have to be honest; he was handsome, and tall, although not as tall as I had imagined a superstar to be. And he had a friendly smile and an enormous head. As he was about to leave, he asked for a business card. He surprised me because as soon as he got in the car, he called the office for me and asked me to go to lunch with him. I met him for lunch and that initial conversation was the sincerest talk I have ever had. He didn't tell me what he was going through. Everything was positive. He was funny. I enjoyed him and he made me laugh and made me smile. Not too many people can do that.

Over time, I let him in my heart. Still, I knew nothing about his indictment or upcoming trial. The following year, I found out about his troubles. He didn't volunteer the information. I had a car accident in his Corvette and I noticed he wasn't able to get his car back, although he had insurance. That didn't feel right. My woman's intuition kicked in. Turns out they repossessed it. I thought back and realized he also wasn't going to the gym and working out. That was odd. Plus, it seemed like he was clubbing all the time. I realized he had money issues.

One day at my apartment, I asked questions. Hedake told me what was going on. He more than said the words; he cried. I had never seen that side of him. He also confessed that he was going through a state of depression. It really got to me when he said he had thought about committing suicide. People who counsel or work with others who say they are considering suicide will tell you, "Talking about suicide is not a call for attention, but a cry for help." Through his apparent pain and agony, I knew he was reaching out to me and crying out for help.

I searched for the right words to say to console him. What do you say when somebody tells you something like that? I held him in my arms. More than that, I cradled him like a baby.

"You know you can't allow that to happen to you. I'm here for you. God is in control, no matter what you have done. You must continue to pray about it and know He'll get you through it," I promised him. I didn't think any different of him. Everyone makes mistakes, but it shocked me to know it was as that serious.

My relationship with God was not nearly as strong as it is now, but it was an important part of my life. My mother, who serves as a minister of music, raised me in the church. But as they say, "You have to work out your own soul's salvation." For a while, I was in and out of church, but in high school, I began to know God for myself. It was something I felt I needed. I developed a close relationship with Him and understood how important it was to have God in my life. When I had my daughter, I knew I needed to change some characteristics about myself in order to be a good example for her. Of course, I needed to work on some of my actions, but God eventually became the center of my life.

When Hedake told me about being involved in a point-shaving scandal, he didn't or couldn't explain everything to me. I investigated on my own and I looked up the term. Mainly, I believed it had to be something earth-shattering if he had contemplated suicide. I discovered in organized sports, point-shaving is a form of match-fixing where the aim is to change the final score of a game without altering the outcome, as stated by Google. "This is typically done by players colluding with gamblers to prevent a team from covering a published point spread, where gamblers bet on the margin of victory."

The more I looked, the more I learned that point-shaving wasn't a new fad. It has been around a long time. Point-shaving differs from purposely losing a game. It involves ensuring that your team does not exceed the point spread. One way this happens in basketball is by allowing mistakes to occur throughout the game—such as missed layups, erroneous passes, and errant free throws. The City College of New York won its NCAA championship in 1950, although being involved in a point-shaving scandal. The consequent investigation showed 32 players from seven colleges admitted to taking bribes between 1947 and 1950 to fix 86 games in 17 states. Unfortunately for those caught partaking in this activity, it's recognize as a federal offense under NCAA rules.

I also saw basketball wasn't the only sport that involved point-shaving. It has happened in almost every sport. On some occasions, it wasn't even for money; it was for party favors. The information I found out surprised me, but not really. Hedake faced federal time because of his involvement in the matter. It shocked me they could take the punishment for such an offense to that level. I believed they wanted to make an example of him. Without hesitation, I supported him wholeheartedly and stood with him during his time of need. Leaving Hedake, walking out, and kicking him to the curb, never entered my mind. Rules are rules, but he didn't rob anybody, and he certainly didn't kill anybody. I didn't even think for one second to drop him because I knew God placed us in each other's life for a reason.

I needed to know how I could help him deal with it. Basketball was important to him, and I wouldn't take that away from him. But it was also important to know everything he faced in order for him to move forward. He needed somebody to help him get through it. By this time, I had deep feelings for him. I felt in my heart he was a nice guy who had made a mistake. Even Jesus said, "Let he who is without sin cast the first stone." As more and more about the case came out, it seemed to me, though, *somebody* had to pay. *Somebody* had to be a scapegoat.

He confided in me about ASU and the boosters, but opted not to incriminate others for a lighter sentence. Like a man, he accepted what he did. We lived together in DeSoto, Texas, about 20 minutes from Dallas. It was a small town of a little over 30,000 people and most of them knew nothing about the scandal. Mostly, Hedake told no one about his ordeal. Even the friend who introduced us didn't know. The television and newspaper interviews and articles came out after he pled guilty. That turned out to be a blessing in disguise.

It was a challenge for me to see him broken down. He was Mr. Personality, the one who knew how to make people laugh and how to make them smile. Eventually, the word got out, and some people's actions were hateful and cruel towards him. At public events, people made negative comments about him.

At some places his "friends" made snide remarks. That broke me more than him. I was fit to be tied. He was going through a heavy situation, and he had to endure actions like this from people he knew.

The most challenging part of this ordeal for me was being there in a way he needed me to be. My biggest concern was I had a child, and I needed to make good choices for her. But when he met her, he instantly fell in love with her and he always treated her like she was his own daughter. The decision to be there for him was not only about me, but about her as well. Then I saw him go through a state of depression. He drank a lot, and he wasn't the person I knew. It hurt to see him like that.

As a Christian woman, I took a liking to him. Not for who he was or what other people saw, but because of the person I knew. What kind of person would I be to leave knowing he needed help to get through what was possibly the most trying time of his life?

If anyone had criticized me for staying with him, I wouldn't have listened, anyway. I make my own decisions and I don't get too involved in what everyone thinks about anything. I talk to God about anything I deal with. But my family loved him, and they understand people make mistakes. There was no judgment from me and none from them.

When we first started dating, people said I was with him for his money. I would ask, "What money?" If they only knew the true extent of his circumstances. I did, and I was still there. There wasn't an ulterior motive, and no one forced me to be with him. I was there because I wanted to be. When we met, I was living on my own with my daughter, so it wasn't like I needed him to pay for anything.

When he pled guilty in Phoenix, Arizona, I was right there by his side. I supported him as they sentenced him to one year and a day in federal prison. We were pleased to see Arizona behind us, and he had a short period to settle his affairs before going to the Federal Correctional Institution in Big Spring, Texas. District Judge Robert C. Broomfield ordered him to surrender to federal authorities by December 13 to serve his sentence.

The sentence was a relief because now he knew what the consequences were for what he did. He could focus on what he needed to do to prepare to have a plan in place when he got released. The big idea was to move forward with his life.

The prison was about four and a half hours from DeSoto. I felt blessed that out of the 122 federal prisons in the US, he was only a short drive from my home. I could visit him all the time. Therefore, I visited the prison along with another young lady whose husband was there as well. We all became friends. She drove one weekend and I drove the next one. Sometimes I went by myself. Hedake called me whenever he could, and we wrote letters back and forth. He also sent me cards. My family, who supported me throughout the experience, made a difficult time somewhat easier. They had a positive influence on our situation, mainly because they liked him and felt he was being railroaded. They too believed he was a good guy who got caught up in an unpleasant situation.

My job was to be there for him emotionally, physically, and in any sense he needed me. I also tried to be understanding that his life changed in a way he couldn't understand. No matter what the obstacle was, I admonished him to stay prayed up and seek God. It wasn't over for him, and I had his back like none other. The nine and a half months he served seemed a lot longer. I missed his company, of course, and it was a different experience. Yet, I continued to talk to God about it and stayed in church to help us get through it. Some people say the time he served was a slap on the wrist. Others say they could have done that in their sleep, especially at a federal prison. The bottom line is, it was still a prison. He, like many black men, was on lockdown. And the time he served gave me a lot to think about and research concerning societal ills and the US prison system.

People often say, "Don't do the crime if you can't do the time." On the surface, that sounds right and politically correct. It would seem the system works, but many of us know someone who is doing 20, 30, 40, or 50, years; and almost every week, we read about someone being released from prison for being wrongly incarcerated. Racial disparity in the US prison system is an ongoing issue throughout the nation. African Americans comprise just 13% of the total population, but make up nearly 40% of those incarcerated. Racial discrimination and systemic bias have caused a disproportionate incarceration rate for African Americans.

They often imprison African Americans for drug possession and shoplifting because of financial difficulties. Research shows that African American men receive harsher punishments than white men for similar crimes. Parole violations amplify the racial gap, resulting in almost half of US federal prisoners being charged with non-violent drug offenses. This can lead to repeated incarcerations because of minor non-violent offense violations while released on parole. Minorities may go to jail for violating parole conditions even if they didn't commit new crimes.

Studies suggests that African Americans are especially likely to be incarcerated for certain crimes. It is my belief that the US justice system must work towards addressing this racial disparity in order to create a fairer and more equitable society. Discussing this issue can lead to meaningful change in the criminal justice system. Until we tackle poverty, injustice, and suffering, our communities will always be affected.

Of course, it excited me when he got out. Physically, he had become cut, and he looked fantastic. He appeared happy, as though he was ready for a new start. I couldn't wait to pick up where we left off in our relationship, in the free world.

The entire experience taught me how much your life can change at the drop of a dime. Again, we all make mistakes. Some of them change the trajectory of our lives. How we get through those blunders makes all the difference in the world. It also taught me that a lot of things that we go through are not about us, but so that your story can help other people. Finally, it taught me material things are not important. You can lose everything you have in a moment, in the blink of an eye.

We had to start over, but we weren't some starry-eyed couple living in a state of Pollyanna. We knew our relationship would be difficult; however, I had some good examples in my family to emulate. There were people like my grandparents, who were married for 63 years before my grandfather passed away. My parents have been married 40 something years. It wouldn't be easy, mainly because we were young. However, if two people commit themselves to being there for each other, they must open themselves up to each other. They must accept the task and be ready for what comes with it.

When Hedake was released from prison, they allowed him to go to a halfway house, and he got a job with my father. That satisfied the parole requirements. The entire ordeal cemented and grew my relationship with God. He is at the forefront of every decision I make. The biggest change is that my attitude towards things and people is different. I've become a lot more patient and understanding. I know there is always a story behind the story that led to them being in the situation they are in.

We've experienced hardships way past what people know about the point-shaving ordeal. We lost every single possession we had, even after he got a second chance. That could have left us bitter, but it made us better. If none of this had happened; if he made it to the NBA, there would be a Hedake story, but maybe not one where people would see God's hand in it. This authentic narrative gives an opportunity for God to be glorified in the end. As far as his story is concerned, it is bigger than any basketball he could have ever bounced because it will glorify God.

It's funny the way God operates. I didn't have to wonder what it was like to be behind bars because I found out for myself. The police put me in jail because of an automobile. We tried to keep our house and other possessions, but I was the only one working because of his career-ending injury. And I wasn't making six figures. Many of the things we had we could not afford. In time, we received letters about one of the vehicles from the finance company.

My attitude was, "You can come and get the car. You know where I live."

One day at work, I received a call from Human Resources. I was told to come to the office and bring all my possessions. When I made it there, a constable was behind the door waiting for me like I was on a Most Wanted list. The HR rep had fear written all over her face. The Irving Police told the constable to take me to Dallas. Every person I came in contact with in Dallas asked, "What are you in here for?" Then they would say something like, "You don't look like you're supposed to be in here."

On the way to take my booking photo, someone called my name.

"DD?" It was the mother of one of my cousin's children.

"What are you doing in here?" she asked incredulously. Before I answered, she said, "I got you."

Time went by and they had not called me to the back. I couldn't post bail until I saw the judge, and it looked like I wouldn't be able to see a judge because of the lateness of the hour. That meant I would have to spend the night.

Eventually, she said, "You're actually supposed to be going to get booked and go to a holding cell, but I will not let them take you back there. I'm going to get a deputy to go with you to where the men are being held. You will be okay. This is for you to see the judge, get a bond, and get out of here."

However, the judge read my charges and said, "No bond." All the men in there were confused.

The deputy came to get me and he walked me out. He said apparently the judge was confused, and he also asked the question, "What did you do?"

"It's a long story. I'm not supposed to be in here, but it is what it is."

Someone eventually changed the order, and I bonded out. Then I hired an attorney. I couldn't work because my job wouldn't let me come back until the case was closed. I tried to get another job during that time, but because I had an open case, no one would hire me.

My attorney talked to the prosecutor, and she read the charges to the grand jury.

He said, "You know what they're going to do," and that's exactly what happened." They dropped the charges.

My faith became stronger because we could get back on our feet. I don't know what God was sending us through, but I never questioned it, either. The journey hasn't been easy. Although I never left, to be completely transparent, sometimes I felt like I wanted to walk away. Some people may have thought I was stupid for standing by him, not knowing if he would have done the same for me, but I'm different. I follow my heart and what God instills in it. I may not understand the road or the path, but I realize we won't always understand. In the end, it is about the obedience and He allows us to experience things in life and the result is that He gains the glory.

Overall, I believe Stevin had to go through this chapter in his life because God wouldn't have gotten glory through him being a star NBA player. He says all the time he thinks he would have been a terrible person because of the pedestal people placed him on.

******

The Bible teaches us that losing something in one realm can actually help us gain in another. We see this again and again throughout the Bible. For example, Jesus taught, "Whoever wants to be my disciple must deny themselves and take up their cross daily and follow me" (Luke 9:23). Jesus was asking His followers to give up all worldly possessions in order for them to inherit eternal life. Apostle Paul further emphasizes this concept when he states, "I have been crucified with Christ and I no longer live, but Christ lives in me" (Galatians 2:20). Here, Paul suggests giving up our earthly life for a spiritual one will bring greater rewards in the end.

In a similar way, the Bible encourages us to surrender our will to God's plan rather than our own. This can mean sacrificing desires or ambitions in order to experience genuine joy and peace by following God's lead. As Proverbs 16:3 tells us, "Commit to the Lord whatever you do and he will establish your plans."

By living according to God's will rather than our own preferences and selfishness, we can gain more than if we had only sought after our own goals. Embracing the biblical lesson of losing to gain can lead to a more fulfilling life. I agree with DD; we have won *way* more than we have lost.

Delicia and Stevin on their wedding day.

CHAPTER 13: NEVER WOULD HAVE MADE IT

It may be possible to gild pure gold, but who can make his mother more beautiful?"
—Mahatma Gandhi

The LORD is my shepherd; I shall not want. (Psalm 23:1)

I knew this day would come, but I didn't think it would ever happen. Yes, that's a contradiction, however, that's exactly how I always felt. I believed my mother would always be here, although I knew intellectually, that wasn't possible. All of us are born to die. Enter, Tuesday, August 1, 2023. It's another one of those dates that, for me, will always live in infamy. As long as I live, I will never forget it.

The previous chapter centered on losing in order to win. August 1, 2023, almost made me want to go back and delete it out of the book. My understanding as I finish this long-awaited manuscript is nil. How can one gain a victory by a loss so momentous that nothing else I have lost can compare to it? Not even losing a career in the NBA and the fame and millions that come with it can measure up to the pain of losing your mother.

People often talk about an incomparable mother's love. Some only talk about it in terms of things they have heard. I lived it. Of course, I'm not saying I'm the only one who knows; I'm only speaking my truth for how I feel about my mother. Courtney Bunn, a lifestyle blogger, states, "A mother's love is limitless." Ironically, on August 1, three years earlier, she wrote, "A mother's love transcends all boundaries. It has the strength to protect, the power to nourish, and the ability to heal. A mother's love is a mighty force that helps transform our world. By providing this love to our children, we can instill an ability to love in them."

I must concur with her. In the quiet corners of my heart, a profound sorrow lingers, and it has much to do with what I learned about love from my mother. Anyone who knows me knows how much I love my mother. I have endured an unimaginable loss, a devastating blow that has shattered my world. In the depths of my grief, I mourn the passing of the one person who was both my pillar of strength and the embodiment of unconditional love—my mother, Eunice M. Smith. I called her EMS, but that moniker didn't mean Emergency Medical Services. Yet, she was always there to help when I was in danger, to snatch me back from the sure jaws of defeat. My journey through life changed unexpectedly because of her death due to cancer. And that caused me to feel grief, loss, and, to a great extent, abandonment.

Although I know the Word of God, however, in my mental battle with the ever-present question of "Why?"... scriptures sometimes ring hollow. Take Ecclesiastes 3:1-8 for an example:

> There is a time for everything,
> and a season for every activity under the heavens:
> a time to be born and a time to die,
> a time to plant and a time to uproot,
> a time to kill and a time to heal,

a time to tear down and a time to build,
a time to weep and a time to laugh,
a time to mourn and a time to dance,
a time to scatter stones and a time to gather them,
a time to embrace and a time to refrain from embracing,
a time to search and a time to give up,
a time to keep and a time to throw away,
a time to tear and a time to mend,
a time to be silent and a time to speak,
a time to love and a time to hate,
a time for war and a time for peace.

Really? A time to die? A time to weep? A time to mourn? If it wouldn't sound sacrilegious, I would ask God, "What were you thinking when You included those words in Your Holy Bible?"

My answer to anyone who asked me how I'm doing is, "I'm good." And I am because I know she's in a better place. The problem for me is, she's not here with me.

He maketh me to lie down in green pastures: he leadeth me beside the still waters. (Psalm 23:2)

From the beginning, my mother and I shared a profound connection. As I stated before, I was born and reared as an only child in a single-parent household, and our bond went beyond the ordinary. People who could not comprehend it, often found themselves battling twinges of jealousy. It was hard for most people to understand our alliance. Our lives intertwined in a delicate dance of love, support, and understanding. My mother never gave up on me and was always there to support me. We created cherished memories that will forever be etched in my soul as we celebrated milestones and weathered storms together.

I've come to the realization that God has a way of sending you signs or signals of what is to come. This one thought was over my head. Before finding out my mother was sick, my wife and I went looking at land with our parents in mind.

It weighed heavy on us that our parents were getting older and we wanted to find a place where my mother and my wife's parents could be comfortable if they would ever need to live with us. Bear in mind, we thought and talked in the future tense, not knowing what was about to hit us head on.

About two weeks after our conversation, my cousin, Shun, took Mama to the hospital and she was eventually checked into Methodist Charlton Medical Center overnight. When they kept her, instead of rushing up there, I decided to go to church first, the place I knew I could find solace. What better place could I be?

After the church service, I went to visit her. As I stepped into her room, my heart sank at the sight before me. I saw my mother lying there, vulnerable and unaware of what was going on with her body. A wave of concern and worry washed over me as I grappled with the stark reality of her condition. We waited a long time to get the final diagnosis. In the meantime, they initially told us that gallstones were responsible. They needed to do a biopsy because they saw a mass on her liver during one of her scans.

They ran many tests and we waited a grueling 13 days for an answer. I must admit, those 13 days were the most frustrating of my life. I was overwhelmed and didn't believe the doctors were forthcoming, with the exception of the consulting oncologist. The nurses and other staff members treated us beautifully, though. In my mind, the doctors suffered from a communication disorder. It's possible everyone feels a certain way when their loved ones are suffering, but this was my mother and I struggled. I wanted to help, yet I was at a loss and no one in authority seemed interested in my situation. It was as if my mother was just a number, another clog in the multibillion-dollar hospital system's wheel.

He restoreth my soul: he leadeth me in the paths of righteousness for his name's sake. (Psalm 23:3)

Methodist is a renowned acute care and teaching hospital in Dallas, yet it meant nothing to me at that point. Their top quality medical services and nationally recognized education and residency programs didn't interest me. They could skip the PR talk about how they provide exceptional care for complex medical conditions that made them famous. All I cared about at that moment was my mama.

Finally, I asked, "Y'all can't tell me anything?" I threatened, "I need to move my mom." Suddenly, answers seemed to appear out of nowhere. The answers might not have been what I wanted to hear, but I finally got a response.

The doctor stoically told us, "The mass is cancerous."

Cancer was back with a vengeance, and no one saw it coming. The news struck like a thunderbolt; I reeled with disbelief and ached with anguish. I stood by her side throughout her valiant battle, and I witnessed the toll it took on her physical and mental well-being. My heart broke a little more with each passing day.

We knew cancer had stealthily invaded my mother's body and my world was completely turned upside down once again. As stated in a previous chapter, this wasn't the first time it had reared it's ugly head. EMS was a fighter, a cancer survivor whose colon cancer had been in remission for almost 30 years.

She had probably been to the hospital twenty times. They never kept her or provided her genuine relief. We would get her home only to hear her say, "I feel like this or I feel like that." Many times, we rushed to the hospital only to be told it was nothing. I always said to DD, "I don't like it, but we're going, anyway."

Yea, though I walk through the valley of the shadow of death, I will fear no evil: for thou art with me; thy rod and thy staff they comfort me (Psalm 23:4).

It took the presence of gallstones to find out she had cancer. I admit, at this point, I am not happy with the medical industry and I'm less happy with the purveyors of insurance. Everything is a process based on the type of insurance and the amount you have. The availability of tests depends on the type of insurance you have. Administers must approve everything first and that can cause dangerous delays. To me, insurance is the biggest rip-off there is. If things were fair, the government would provide full coverage for all senior citizens, especially those who have worked for 20, 30, and 40 years. But that's how I think. Everyone else has a right to think the way they do. Just don't go into the hospital as a common person.

With health insurance for Americans over 65, the most common choice is Medicare. This federally funded insurance program is specifically for those 65 and older and meets the criteria. Medicare comprises two primary parts - Part A, also known as Hospital Insurance, and Part B, which covers Medical Insurance. Although Medicare provides valuable coverage, it does not encompass 100% of all costs! Ask around and it might surprise you at the number of people you discover who must decide each month between food or medicine. Our elderly should not have to live like that.

I made it my business to visit my mother every day. Not only because that's what I should do as a son, but also because I wanted the hospital staff to stay on their toes. I needed them to see somebody cared about Eunice M. Smith. When I look back at the situation, the way it happened, I could see she was deteriorating. She was really sick.

The days slowly ticked by. I had one of those wait-a-minute-what's-going-on? moments. She was still in the hospital and I watched them take blood from her day after day. I witnessed her hands as they changed color. I couldn't do my ordinary routine. For the first time since we started our trucking company, I didn't worry about the trucks running. Income took a distance second place. My undivided attention was on my mother and what we had to do for her to be all right. And that one day turned into her being in the hospital for 16 days.

She became weak because she wasn't eating. To help keep her strength up, the doctors ordered liquids and liquid foods. She also needed a PET Scan to determine where the cancer originated. After a while, they wanted to discharge her to a facility, but if she went to a facility, she couldn't see the oncologist and almost no one else as an inpatient.

DD said, "If she is going to be discharged, she is going home with us." DD wanted us to schedule any appointments my mother needed; especially the ones for the PET Scan and oncologist. You have got to love someone like that. Before I even brought it up, she had already decided.

My mother was supposed to be discharged on Monday, but she came down with pneumonia. Instead of getting out on that day, she stayed another four days in the hospital, then she finally came home. The plan called for me, my wife, and daughters, to give her around the clock care. We built a support system that included my daughters, Aerian, Kayla, and Chloé; my uncle,

Ural; my cousin, Shun; and my goddaughters. And that also included initiating lifestyle changes for us. For example, we had never ordered food from Sprouts.com, but it became a staple in our house. DD researched and recommended that we include organic food in our diet. We did so, although it was a challenge, like everything else.

To be truthful, the entire ordeal of being caregivers was a challenge, one that I would gladly undergo 1000 times if I had to. In the corner of my heart lives an indescribable journey—one filled with moments of both despair and hope; a journey that forever changed my perspective on life, love, and loss. It was the path of caregiver to my terminally ill parent, a role that stretched the limits of my strength and resilience, although it was only for a short period.

I found comfort in my family during those times. My wife did things for my mother that were difficult for me to process. Her enduring support, from late-night conversations to gentle embraces, provided a lifeline when I felt I could no longer carry on. My youngest daughter, Chloé, at age 19, was mature beyond her years. She cleaned her, bathed her, and made her comfortable. Her tender smiles and innocent laughter reminded me of the beauty that remained amidst the pain. My other daughters stepped up to help wherever they could. It was the continuous love of our support system that provided the greatest source of strength. Their presence was a beacon of hope, illuminating the darkest corners of our journey. Their love propelled me forward, giving me the strength to face each day anew.

As we took on the responsibility of caring for my mother, a sense of dread washed over me. The burden of witnessing her pain and suffering was immense, but I knew I had to be there for her, every step of the way. Days blurred into nights, and nights into endless vigils. Together, we navigated the complexities of medical treatments and emotional uncertainties. The weight of this undertaking threatened to consume me, and it tested my resolve at every turn. Yet, amid the darkness, I discovered the strength to endure.

Though heartache marked our journey, the unbreakable bond of love that carried us through ultimately defined it. And in that love, we found solace, hope, and the strength to face each new day, knowing that we were never alone.

When you care for a loved one, time seems to stand still, but your life must go on. The last weekend in July, DD and I went to San Antonio to celebrate our 21st anniversary. It just so happened that we also had a delivery to make and planned to come back Sunday night. We decided to "kill two birds with one stone," so to speak. Traveling four hours away wasn't a simple decision. However, it was important for us to acknowledge and celebrate another year of marriage. Making a little money in the process was the icing on the cake. We weren't overly concerned about leaving because we had a great support system around us. Uncle Ural, my mother's brother, came to DeSoto and stayed with her for the weekend.

However, my mother had been saying all weekend that she felt like she needed to burp, but she couldn't. On Sunday night, she started having problems. We arrived back home a little after midnight.

When daylight came around, we had to leave to get her medicine and other items. Still wanting to get some relief for her stomach, she asked DD to have one of our daughters bring her a Coke. As many people know, carbonated beverages, such as soda or fizzy drinks, contain carbon dioxide that dissolves in the liquid. When consumed, the dissolved carbon dioxide transforms into a gas that can lead to belching. But that's when all hell broke loose. She vomited. Chloé called us to say she was calling 911. She said GiGi threw up all over herself and it was black. My wife told her we were around the corner, literally one minute away. When we made it home and walked through the door, I wasn't the nicest human being, and my daughter received the brunt of my frustration.

"What's wrong with you? You don't have to call us for something like that. Call 911!" I shouted. In her defense, she was already prepared to call 911, but wanted to inform us what had transpired first. The Coke Kayla brought her allowed my mother to do what she had tried to do all weekend; burp. We surmised it resulted from something she ate. But the black phlegm was concerning along with the large red blood clots. One paramedic pulled me to the side and told me she was likely bleeding on the inside, and it indicated potential liver failure.

This time, we had the ambulance take her to Methodist Medical Center on Colorado. After we arrived, I realized it was the same hospital where my grandmother, my mother's mother, died.

She was in so much pain when she got there; they kept her and ran tests. It turned out the black stuff she was throwing up was indeed blood, as the paramedics stated.

On August 1, I can't say I knew her time was near, but I felt at peace. I was comfortable enough to leave to take care of some personal business. I wasn't gone long, maybe three hours, when I received a call from my wife. "Stevin, she's gone," DD said. And with those three words, my whole life changed.

When the moment arrived to say goodbye, I felt a profound emptiness settle within me, a void that could never be filled. The aftermath of losing my mother left me drowning in a sea of emotions. Grief washed over me in waves, threatening to consume my every breath. The pain of abandonment and the haunting feeling of loneliness became constant companions. But amid the darkness, flickers of cherished memories emerged, providing fragments of solace. To cope with my overwhelming emotions, I sought peace in the support of friends and family. Their open arms and compassionate hearts offered a lifeline in my darkest hours.

Thou preparest a table before me in the presence of mine enemies: thou anointest my head with oil; my cup runneth over. (Psalm 23:5)

The celebration of life began with a viewing on August 11, at Eternal Rest Funeral Home in DeSoto. It concluded on August 12 at St. John Missionary Baptist Church in Oak Cliff. I asked God to give me strength, and that's what I'm amazed about. I cried when she was in the hospital, but once she transitioned, I never shed a tear. At the funeral, my heart rejoiced when Chloé praise danced to the song, "I Shall Wear A Crown."

That's a powerful song that carries deep symbolism and meaning. It's often associated with spirituality and religion, particularly in African American gospel culture. The lyrics of the song express a strong sense of hope, triumph, and perseverance in the face of adversity. The crown mentioned in the song represents a symbol of victory, honor, and eternal reward. It conveys the idea that we may experience challenges and struggles in life; however, there is a promise of ultimate triumph and glory. "I Shall Wear a Crown," serves as a reminder to hold on to faith, endure hardships, and remain steadfast in pursuing righteousness and salvation. This message inspires listeners to find their inner strength and strive for greatness, knowing they will be successful in the end. I sat there among the solemn atmosphere at my mother's funeral. A whirlwind of emotions engulfed me and took me on an emotional roller-coaster I had never expected. My mother was more than a parent to me; she was my confidante, my rock, and my biggest cheerleader. She was always there for me with warm hugs, laughter, and late-night conversations, and she guided me with love and wisdom.

Her passing hit me like a tidal wave, and the magnitude of the loss slowly settled in. A mixture of shock, disbelief, and overwhelming grief consumed my entire being. It felt as if time stood still, and the world around me faded into a blur. Joyous and bittersweet memories of her flooded my mind.

Thankfully, the funeral service was a celebration of my mother's life. My mother-in-law sang one of my mother's favorite songs, "There's a Leak in This Old Building." The funeral director adorned the setting with fragrant flowers that filled the air with their sweet scent. Soft, melancholic melodies played in the background and created a beautiful atmosphere. Friends and family gathered; their faces etched with sadness, but also with a shared sense of gratitude for having known my mother.

The eulogies and speeches painted a vivid picture of my mother's impact on the lives of those around her. Stories of her selflessness, kindness, and undying support brought smiles through the tears. I heard incidents of how she had touched the lives of others, offered a helping hand, lent a listening ear, and spread joy wherever she went.

Seeing friends and acquaintances show love and support made me feel happy and sad at the same time. People offered us compassion and companionship, and proved her profound influence. Their gestures of condolences, warm embraces, and shared memories offered peace in this difficult time. As I reflect on the emotional highs and lows I experienced during my mother's funeral, I realize the immeasurable impact she had on all of us. Her legacy lives on through the lives she touched, the love she shared, and the memories she left behind. Although the pain is unbearable, I find comfort in knowing that her spirit will forever live on within me and in the hearts of those she loved.

Surely goodness and mercy shall follow me all the days of my life: and I will dwell in the house of the LORD for ever. (Psalm 23:6)

As I embark on a new chapter of my life without my mother's physical presence, I carry her spirit within me. I find peace in cherishing the memories we shared, recounting our laughter, our conversations, and our unbreakable bond. Though my heart aches, I draw strength from the lessons she imparted, the values she instilled, and the love she showered upon me. In honoring her legacy, I discover the resilience to forge ahead, and embrace the world with a renewed sense of purpose. Faced with adversity, hope emerges like a fragile bud in spring. I, though forever altered by her loss, will learn to navigate the uncharted waters of my grief. I carry forward her memory, weaving it into the tapestry of my life and find peacefulness in pursuing the dreams we once shared and comfort in the legacy she left behind. And while the pain may never fully dissipate, I am determined to honor her by living a life filled with love, compassion, and resilience.

Heart-wrenching sorrow marks my journey, but also I embrace an everlasting love that withstands the test of time. As I navigate the uncharted territory of my new reality, memories allows me to embrace the hope that springs from honoring her legacy. In my heart, I carry my mother's love forever, a guiding light that will illuminate my path as I forge ahead into a new chapter of life.

To this day, we still don't know where the cancer originated. Even with having the death certificate, it wasn't clear. When I read the death certificate on August 23, I finally cried, but they were tears of joy. According to the certificate, she had internal bleeding for two days, but had suffered for weeks. I was glad her pain and sorrow were over.

EMS shares a tender moment with her son, Stevin.

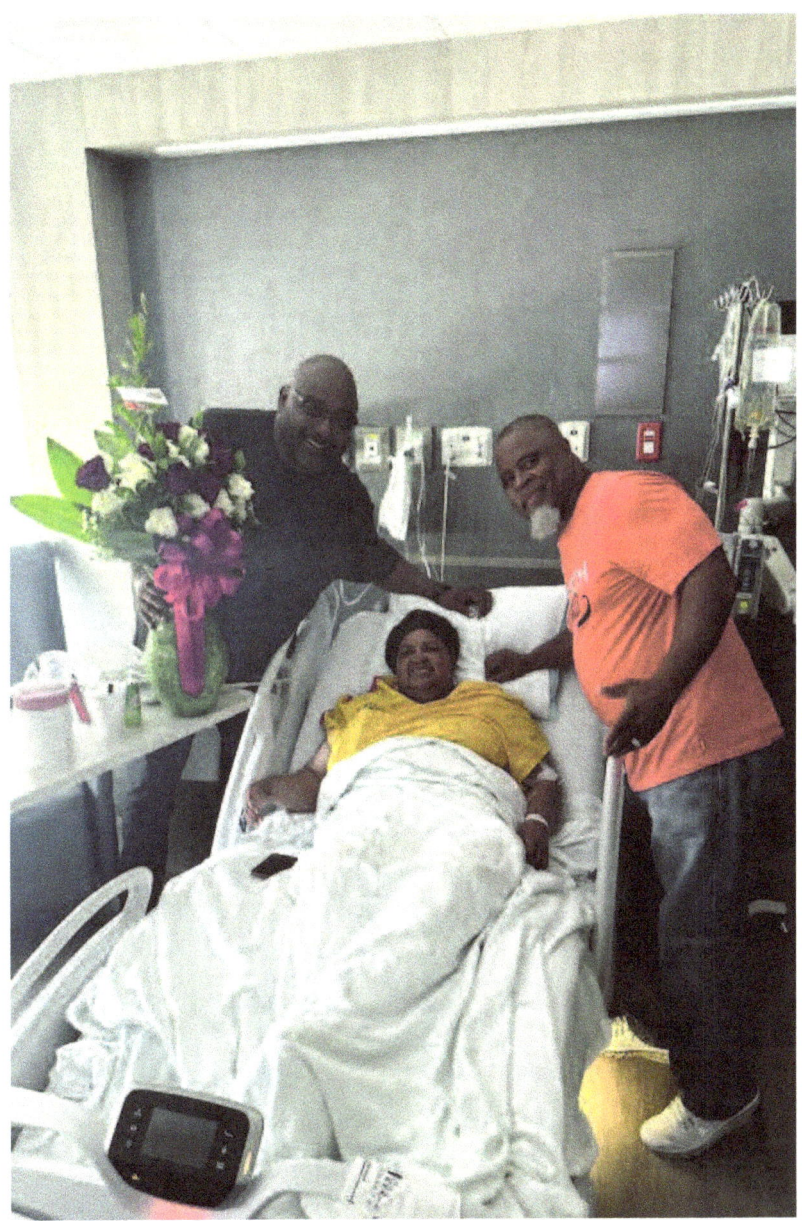

At the hospital, Stevin surprised his mother with flowers, personally delivered by David Snell, owner of Butterflies and Snails.

EPILOGUE

I always keep my headlights on, whether I'm traveling in broad daylight or in darkness. That way, folks can see me as I emerge or come from behind. When it rains outside, I laugh, because I know from personal experience storms don't last forever. I am a living and breathing testimony of this and much more.

As I've said time and time again, everybody makes mistakes in life. But as I've learned, suffered, grown, and matured, now I know the only thing wrong with making mistakes and falling down, is not getting back up. Besides, if I didn't make the mistakes I made in my life, I wouldn't have this testimony to share with you—my readers, fans, supporters and critics. The mistakes I made are a part of who I am now and what I feel God has ultimately purposed me for.

Except for the people I may have hurt or disappointed along the way with my actions and choices, I have learned to live with no regrets. I am not bitter about being stripped of my accolades. Neither am I bitter about the fact many basketball coaches have made millions from successful basketball programs. Many of them flourished because of players, like me, who did the work but received little financial reward in return. I still feel the need to set the record straight.

From my experience, I can tell you how easily players can get drawn into fixing games. Poor, naïve teenagers, combined with rich, greedy gamblers, is a recipe for disaster. If for no other reason than this, I wanted to tell my story, and hope the next player who gets enticed may think twice and make the right decision. In the end, I did my time, paid my fines, and served 9 1/2 months in prison.

Yet, sometimes it appears society and the world gave me a life sentence. In the past, I must admit, I felt sorry for myself. Some days I become disappointed and down. Especially when I think about the fact that my wife and daughters, may never see me named to the Basketball Hall of Fame. However, I am proud to say I am still blessed. My records will stand on their own. I can't erase my past, but I strive to be better than I used to be. Although I am not officially listed anywhere as a Hall of Famer, I know I will always hold a place in God's "Hall of Fame." And that's because of who I am, where I came from, and who He created me to be. The name Stevin "Hedake" Smith speaks for itself. People still desire my No. 44 ASU college jersey, and my accomplishments and body of work as a basketball player speaks for themselves.

On the baseline of the court at the American Airlines Center in Dallas, my name sits. Listed are all the ex-Mavericks players and, although I only played for 20 days, I am counted among them. And I'm still here. No one can erase my legacy. I can learn from my faults and get wisdom from those willing to give it. But most of all, I have a family who loves me, and a God who loves me even more, and that is something money can't buy. It's been a journey and a glorious ride, and I'm much obliged for all of it. When I think back on the 52 years of life God has blessed me with, I think of Zacardi Cortez. He's one of my favorite Gospel artists, who puts it best when he says in his song, "You Don't Know:"

> *My Father never lets me down. He's always around,*
> *even when I can't see.*

This song is like the soundtrack of my life. Along with some misfortunes, I fell in love with a game at age five and it allowed me to achieve greatness with God's help. The places He's allowed me to travel, some people will only dream of. Therefore, I am and will always be thankful… to God be the glory.

To My Three Remarkable Daughters: Aerian, Kayla and Chloê

Within these pages lies more than just photographs; they are fragments of time, echoes of laughter, and whispers of love that have filled our home and hearts.

Each image is a testament to the journey we've embarked on together, a journey that has witnessed your growth from playful children to beautiful, God-fearing women.

Your grace, strength, and compassion inspire me daily, and I am endlessly appreciative for the blessing you are in my life.

This section is dedicated to you, not only as a celebration of the moments we've shared but also as a tribute camaraderie to the incredible individuals you have become.

May these memories serve as a reminder of our unbreakable bond and the unconditional love that surrounds us always.

With all my heart,

Dad (Stevin "Hedake" Smith)

Stevin along with his daughters in the earlier years,
Aerian, Chloê, and Kayla.

The Smith family: Aerian, Delicia, Stevin, Chloê, Kayla, and EMS.

The Smith family: Aerian, Chloê, Delicia, Stevin, and Kayla.

Chloê

Kayla

Aerian

AP, Stevin, basketball fan, and Eric in Israel.

Coach Roy Williams, Stevin, and Steve Woodberry.

Stevin and Monty Williams, famed NBA coach.

Kyrie Irving, Stevin, and Nolen Smith.

Stevin in a Spruce High School charity game.

Playing in the Red Bird League, a college summer league.

Stevin in the Philippines.

Stevin as a member of USA basketball.

Pacific Conference publication showing Stevin as ASU's leading scorer.

BIBLIOGRAPHY

1. "1999 Events." Historic Newspapers. https://www.historic-newspapers.com/blog/1999-events/?srsltid=AfmBOooZqv95fTFI5eqBeniWLRMYj3gpC5cwNnBvX-vQZMSR_jD8eb3p.
2. "Crafting the 'Day of Infamy' Speech." National Archives. https://www.archives.gov/publications/prologue/2001/winter/crafting-day-of-infamy-speech.html.
3. "Pro Sports Odds." Scholarship Stats. https://scholarship stats.com/pro-odds.
4. "When Pain, No Gain." Medical Massage EDU. https://www.medicalmassage-edu.com/blog/when-pain-no-gain.htm.
5. "Music Soul R&B Funk Rap Rock N Roll: James Brown." Ima Sportsphile. https://imasportsphile.com/music-soul-r-b-funk-rap-rock-n-roll-james-brown-l-es-stories-special-the-godfather-of-soul-taught-the-world-about-black-music-and-dance-while-developing-several-genres-of-music-i/.
6. "NBA 2K20: 1990s Historic Draft Classes." Crucial Baskets. https://crucialbaskets.com/2020/03/30/nba-2k20-1990s-historic-draft-classes/.
7. "War on Drugs." Britannica. https://www.britannica.com/topic/war-on-drugs.
8. "There Are Always Four Sides to a Story." Quozio. https://quozio.com/quote/drd3mqxm3xqm/1042-25829/there-are-always-four-sides-to-a-story-your-side-their-side.
9. "History of Air Jordan." Foot Locker. https://www.footlocker.com/history-of-air-jordan.html.
10. "All for One and One for All." Quora. https://www.quora.com/Where-did-all-for-one-and-one-for-all-originate.
11. "South Dallas." Wikipedia. https://en.wikipedia.org/wiki/South_Dallas.

12. Vermeer, Hunter. "A Tale of Two Cities: Separation and Contact Between Dallas's Black and White Communities, 1919-1936." https://twu.edu/media/documents/history-government/A-Tale-of-Two-Cities.pdf.
13. "The Jeffersons." IMDb. https://www.imdb.com/title/tt0072519/.
14. "Racial Disparities in Maternal Mortality." PMC. https://pmc.ncbi.nlm.nih.gov/articles/PMC5915910/.
15. Guida, James. "The Lessons of Dr. Funk." The New York Review of Books. https://www.nybooks.com/online/2014/10/22/lessons-of-dr-funk/?srsltid=AfmBOooMoTK1_ove8QW0sXaszf7UKTb3ukUd3xTbtOdqUaL3YhLglkSS.
16. Prince, Zenitha. "Census Bureau: Higher Percentage of Black Children Live with Single Mothers." Afro. December 31, 2016. https://afro.com/census-bureau-higher-percentage-black-children-live-single-mothers/.
17. "YMCA Dallas 2025." OneCause. https://p2p.onecause.com/ymcadallas2025.
18. "Mama, I Want to Sing!" Wikipedia. https://en.wikipedia.org/wiki/Mama,_I_Want_to_Sing!_(film).
19. "No Pass, No Play." Houston Chronicle. https://www.houstonchronicle.com/texas-sports-nation/jenny-dial-creech/article/When-no-pass-no-play-changed-Texas-high-school-14082994.php.
20. "Peer Influence." Raising Children Network. https://raisingchildren.net.au/teens/behaviour/peers-friends-trends/peer-influence.\
21. "Schools Named After Confederate Figures." Education Week. https://www.edweek.org/leadership/data-the-schools-named-after-confederate-figures/2020/06.
22. "H. Grady Spruce High School." Wikipedia. https://en.wikipedia.org/wiki/H._Grady_Spruce_High_School.
23. "A Father-Figure's Support." PMC. https://pmc.ncbi.nlm.nih.gov/articles/PMC4104793/.

24. "UNLV Receives Three Years Probation from NCAA." UPI. https://www.upi.com/Archives/1993/11/09/UNLV-receives-three-years-probation-from-NCAA/5187752821200/.
25. "South Dallas/Fair Park Population." D Magazine. http://neighborhoods.dmagazine.com/dallas/central-dallas/south-dallas-fair-park/.
26. "About Griggs Chapel." Griggs Chapel. https://griggs chapel.com/about/.
27. "D'Angelo." Wikipedia. https://en.wikipedia.org/wiki/D%27Angelo.
28. "10 Facts About the Founding Fathers." American Battlefield Trust. https://www.battlefields.org/learn/articles/10-facts-founding-fathers.
29. "1950 NCAA Basketball Championship Game." Wikipedia. https://en.wikipedia.org/wiki/1950_NCAA_basketball_championship_game.
30. "A Mother's Love Isn't Limited." Promise Prenatal. https://promiseprenatal.com/blogs/news/a-mothers-love-isnt-limited?srsltid=AfmBOopc0_-UXYVS1n95m8c8kbZkucC37AoJH1a-1quNrYb5I6OvJz8P.
31. "Parts of Medicare." Medicare. https://www.medicare.gov/basics/get-started-with-medicare/medicare-basics/parts-of-medicare. basketball_championship_game.

Overcoming Trials and Tribulations: Stevin Hedake Smith's Inspiring Journey

Are you searching for a speaker who can captivate your audience with a powerful story of resilience and redemption? Look no further than Stevin Hedake Smith, the former Arizona State standout who has overcome adversity to become an inspiring role model.

A Journey of Triumph over Adversity

Stevin's journey is one of triumph over adversity. As a young athlete, Stevin became caught up in a point-shaving scandal that shook the sports world. However, instead of letting this setback define him, he used it as a catalyst for personal growth and transformation.

Inspiring Audiences of All Ages

Stevin is now available to speak to a variety of audiences, including churches, corporations, youth groups, and more. His message focuses on overcoming trials and tribulations and becoming the person God wants you to be. Through his compelling storytelling and relatable experiences, Stevin inspires individuals to rise above their own challenges and reach their full potential.

Key Topics Covered

1. **Resilience in the Face of Adversity:** Stevin shares his strategies for bouncing back from setbacks and finding strength in difficult times.
2. **Finding Purpose and Identity:** Stevin delves into his personal journey of self-discovery and offers practical insights into finding one's true purpose.
3. **Building Character and Integrity:** Stevin emphasizes the importance of character and integrity in both personal and professional life. He highlights the positive impact they can have on achieving success.
4. **Overcoming Obstacles:** Stevin provides valuable lessons on overcoming obstacles, navigating through challenges, and embracing change with a positive mindset.
5. **Motivation and Inspiration:** Stevin's captivating storytelling and genuine passion inspire audiences to embrace their own journey towards personal growth and success.

Book Stevin for Your Next Event

Invite Stevin Hedake Smith to speak at your next event. He will provide your audience with a transformative experience. His story will inspire and motivate people to overcome their own struggles.

If you think the book *Hedake* is mesmerizing, hear Stevin Hedake Smith's story live and in person.

To book Stevin Hedake Smith or inquire about speaking opportunities, please contact ssmith@epicglobalsolutions.com. Don't miss this chance to inspire your audience and ignite the spark of resilience within them.

Stevin Hedake Smith gives an inspirational talk at Texas Christian University.

Stevin Hedake Smith poses with Doc Sellers, a former coach at ASU, and Hall of Fame Coach Bill Self at the University of Kansas.

Stevin Hedake Smith with the Texas Christian University basketball team after delivering an inspirational talk.

Patrick McCalla interviews Stevin Hedake Smith for the No Grey Area podcast.

www.ingramcontent.com/pod-product-compliance
Lightning Source LLC
Chambersburg PA
CBHW070401240426
43661CB00056B/2491